VI
Hanoi
Old Quarter

CITY WALKS

PAGE ADDIE PRESS
UNITED KINGDOM. AUSTRALIA

DISCLAIMER

VIETNAM
Hanoi
Old Quarter

CITY WALKS

PAGE ADDIE PRESS
UNITED KINGDOM. AUSTRALIA

CONTENTS

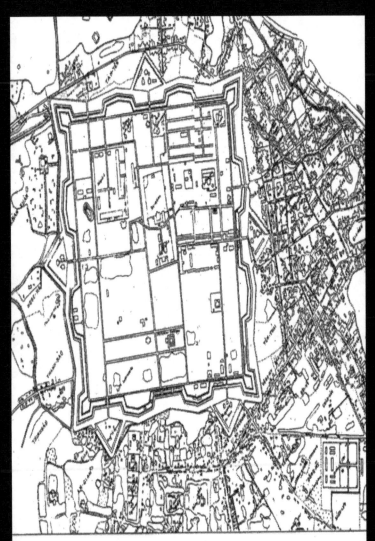

du plan de Hanoi en 1885

WALKING THE ANCIENT STREETS OF HANOI

Have you ever met a friend who told you something that changed the course of your life? We did. Our long-time friend had just come back from Vietnam. He said, if you want to see an old occidental city before it changes, you should go to Hanoi. So we did. We booked a return ticket to Hanoi. Call it serendipity, happenstance or fate, but our six week visit turned into an eight year love affair with with Hanoi. We really know this intense city. We learned simple pleasures from our Vietnamese friends, the warm steam rising from an earthenware cup; how it touches you like a blessing. We spent so long here, our Vietnamese friend says we have the Red River running through our veins! Yes, somehow this strange and unknown oriental city became part of who we are now.

We migrated from our hotel room to an authentic French colonial villa, in a small alley off Da Thuong Street. Located in the French Quarter, the house was a few roads away from the Old Quarter. To get to the Old Quarter we walked past the infamous Maison Centrale Prison, nicknamed The Hanoi Hilton. The famous back streets of the Old Quarter soon became as familiar as the back of our hands. The reason we wrote this guide book is simple. We so often see tourists walking in confusion and frustration. We saw a couple arguing, on Valentine's Day. At the heart of this guidebook, we hope we can save a few relationships between travelling friends!

The longest walk begins with a simple step. We give you tools at your fingertips to walk-it-yourself (instead of paying a tour operator to take you from pillar to pagoda). Instead, create your own personal experience in your own time. When you need to take a break, stop at a street food cafe, sit on a blue plastic stool (a small chair) mingle with the locals, in a real place, where time stops; enjoy what the Vietnamese enjoy - watching their world go by. Yes, we believe our friend was right. Hanoi is one of the last true occidental cities left in Asia.

The information we now share with you, is the same we share with our family and friends. If you are reading this, you will either be packing your bags for your upcoming trip to Hanoi, or unpacking in a local Hanoi hotel and wondering where to go and what to do next.

As with many cities, there's no better way to experience the vibrant street life than by using your own two feet. Walking as a tourist in an ancient Asian city can be exhilarating, exciting and frustrating. When you travel across the world to get here, with a limited time frame, you want to experience the authentic Hanoi. Not knowing what represents authentic experiences can leave you feeling like you have missed seeing the authentic Hanoi.

Much of the energy in Hanoi is packed into thirty six narrow streets, so finding your feet can be a challenge. The streets are busy and noisy, yes. The only time the streets are not busy is during the days of Tet lunar holiday. Stores close, basket women disappear, no rose sellers on bicycles and not a motorbike to be seen. For those few days the streets are quiet and empty. Relaxing, some would say, but to us, the heart of the place goes too.

The Hanoi Old Quarter we know, is a noisy, busy cacophony. This adds emotional depth to the experience. Flash by in a taxi and you'll miss it. You cannot forecast what experiences you will have. One stumbles across them by chance. Doorway to doorway. A continuously changing scene. The Old Quarter is about walking for your senses. A virtual rainbow of colors; embroidered silks; red dragons painted on paper kites; the salty, sweet, sour, hot street foods; exotic hints of camphor, musk, jasmine flowers, ginger, lotus and cinnamon bark; the air filled with songs from tiny birds in bamboo cages; chaotic, frenetic, hustle of the East. It is this intensity that promises to bring back memories of this fascinating occidental city, long after you leave here.

When you are in Asia, life takes place on the streets. We like to think, that with this guide to the Old Quarter, you will walk in the footsteps of a thousand years of Vietnamese traditions. Walking the Old Quarter is a step back into the culture that grew up around the old citadel of Thang Long. You can still see the citadel's main gate and North door located at the intersection of Chu Van An and Nguyen Thai Hoc Street.

The Old Quarter is often called, The 36 Old Guild

Streets. Some believe that the number 36 came from 15th century writings that described 36 administrative units. Another idea is based around the number nine (3+6) which in Asia represents 'plenty', times that by the four directions of north, south, west, east which equals 36. What ever the reason, it's a fascinating city, steeped in living history.

Traditionally the streets were named after the collective trades or guilds in a particular area of the Old Quarter. In effect, these were independent local communities, each having a communal house. Hang Bac Street means Silver Street and Hang Thiec means Tin Street. Streets were also named after kings, poets, generals and heroic revolutionary figures.

Traditionally most of the houses in the Old Quarter are called tube houses. These narrow buildings come from an era where building taxes were based on the area of street frontage. On average, tube houses were 3 - 4 meters wide and 15 - 20 meters long. The front of the house was the place of business and at the back, various rooms and courtyards were used for storage and artisan activity. Beyond the work and storage spaces were living quarters for the family. Often, three generations lived and worked in the same house. The culture is the same today. Grand-parents, parents and children often live at the same address. When a family member passes on, they join the photos on the family alter and are worshiped every day.

The city houses played a strategic part in the national resistance against the French colonists. Internal walls separating the houses often had secret access ways. Patriots could go from one end of the street to the other, secretly moving around the city.

USING THE BOOK

There are seven walking tours in this book. We invite you to choose a walk and follow the map provided to walk from start to finish. The street names are on old French style tin signs, which can be found on buildings and posts in the street. Most of the shops have the street number and name printed on their frontage.

As you go, read the insider information provided to enhance your journey with facts and highlights. If you have just a few days in Hanoi, logistically, you won't be able to walk all the tours in your short time here! Even walking one street with the guide book, gives you an insiders look at the ancient city of Hanoi.

CITY SAFETY

People ask us about safety in Hanoi. As a foreigner, we feel safer walking the streets here, than we did in our cities back home. The laws are strict here and offences against foreign guests are dealt with harshly.

We may be just lucky or careful but we have not had one incidence of theft at our house or on the street. The best advice we can give, is to tune your awareness up a notch in crowded areas. That doesn't necessarily mean clutching your bag to your chest in a paranoid wide-eyed tourist grip. Just use common sense. Carry your wallet in a safe place (not in your back pocket) and be mindful. Make sure bags are closed securely and always in your possession, especially in stores and restaurants. Don't take everything with you as you have too much to lose. Less is best, especially passports. Leave them in a hotel safe. Be aware of your personal space around ATM machines. Don't count your money in public view. If around banks, you may be approached by well-practiced professionals offering to change your foreign currency. Avoid changing money on the streets.

DEFINITIONS

HANG

Merchandise or shop. Hang is often associated to a street name.

DINH

An area allocated to a craft guild. The Dinh (area) usually has one family who takes responsibility for the village guild's temple.

TEMPLE

Situated in a private house. Used by the local community, to worship the village deity and guild ancestors. Normally located on the first floor in the store.

ASSEMBLY HALL

The Chinese traders set up assembly halls for their clan to meet and hold communal discussions. The construction of these halls were overseen by Chinese emissaries from the respective guilds in China. They came specifically to give instructions on the implementation of the right way to do things.

COMMUNAL HOUSE

Traditionally the streets were named after the collective trades or guilds in a particular area of the Old Quarter. In effect, these were independent local communities, each having a communal house. A private house with a temple inside. Used for the communal worship of the village deity.

GUILD

The guild of craftsmen come from a village where the craft has been practiced and the deity worshiped for centuries.

THE WATER PUPPET WALK

LENGTH: 2.5 KILOMETERS. TIME: APPROX 2-3 HOUR WALK.

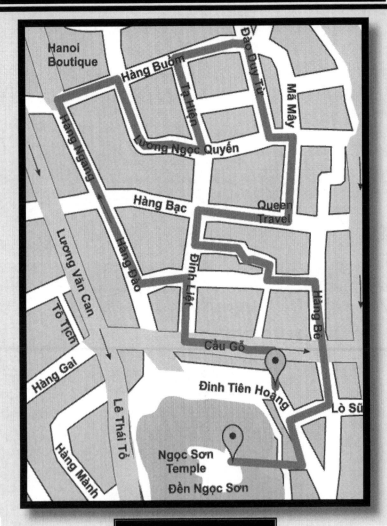

ĐINH TIÊN HOÀNG

This walk begins at the famous Thang Long Water Puppet Theatre located at 57B Dinh Tien Hoang Street. Water puppets are puppets that dance on water. Originating in the 11th century, from villages in the Red River Delta, the traditional stories depict historical and romantic events. When the rice fields flooded, the villagers would entertain each other with water puppets. Puppetry is a secret tradition, that has been passed down through generations. If you want to escape from the heat of a Hanoi day, book a ticket for a show. The atmosphere is calm and refreshing on account of the stage being cool water.

Next door to the theatre, 57B sells famous weasel coffee beans, handmade souvenirs; silk and cotton bags and silk scarves. The shop next to 57B, sells hand painted traditional masks and puppets of the style used in village plays and ceremonies.

Turn left into Cau Go Street.

CÀU GỖ

The name reflects the original function of the street. A wooden bridge was built over an old creek. Then French colonists reclaimed Hang Dao Lake, Taiji Lake and Hoan Kiem Lake tributaries, for land development. The bridge, creek and two lakes all disappeared. Now the only remaining lake is Hoan Kiem.

The first Pho restaurant opened in Hanoi on Cau Go Street. Pho is a famous street food in Vietnam;a noodle soup consisting of broth, rice noodles, fresh herbs, and beef or chicken. Now served in speciality restaurants from Sydney to Paris.

If you want to sample some traditional dishes, Cau Go Street is a popular food mecca. Food is cheap and delicious. Commune with the locals while eating delicious pho; rice or vermicelli with chicken; steamed sticky rice cakes with special herbs, rice cakes filled with meat, onions and mushrooms.

At night, street food stalls and small restaurants offer barbecued seafood, from the port of Hai Phong. For our book on street food, you may like to look on www. amazon.com and type in 'Vietnamese street food translations'. A guide to over 600 street food dishes translated from Vietnamese into English; so you can order food like a local.

Look out for a market lane called Ngo Cau Go off the main street. This is an authentic lane, typical of local Hanoi life. In the early morning, Ngo Cau Go turns into a beloved flower and fresh produce market and presents a feast to the eyes. In the afternoon, vendors sell fresh beef, pork, chicken and often cat-fish, frogs, paddy-field crabs and freshwater snails. Home refrigeration has become more common, but the locals still like to ensure freshness by buying fresh produce every day (if not twice a day) to take home for lunch or evening meals.

At number 43 Cao Co, for the past fifty years, they have been making a famous Hanoi dish called Bun Cha. Small barbecued pork patties served on rice noodles; in a bowl of fragrant broth; side dishes of herb salad; fried spring rolls; garlic and chili pick-les. The spring rolls are seasoned ground meat, mushrooms, and diced carrots, kohlrabi and jicama, rolled up in rice paper; deep fried until crispy. You have to ask the vendor for 'nem gio' (spring rolls). Point to them, hold up your fingers to say how many. Bun Cha is a lunchtime dish served between 11am and 2pm.

Don't be put off by the shabby,dated decor. This style of eating is so local, often you find yourself eating in someone's living room; television tuned into the Vietnamese news; the family alter, roses, oranges and the incense burning. Make yourself at home (but don't stare or take photos of the alter). After mingling with the locals head to Number 73. Popular Avalon Cafe with balconies above the street, sky garden and lake views.

Turn right into Dinh Liet Street.

ĐINH LIỆT

KNITTING STREET

Historically this has been the one stop street for haberdashery. There are still knitting shops for wool, needles, knitted sweaters and scarves. Dinh Liet also has boutique shops specializing in beads, jewelry, silk scarves and bags.

7A Quan Bia Minh is a popular restaurant with expats. The restaurant is upstairs in the old French colonial house where there's a shady veranda and a view down to the street.

Turn left into Gia Ngu Street.

GIA NGU

This area was once a large lake, called Lake Tai Chi. The lake was full of fish, with fish markets along its shores. The water disappeared when the French colonists filled the lake in, as part of the colonial land development plan for Hanoi.

In the last twenty years, it has become famous internationally for its boutique shops for expectant mothers and babies. In the middle of Gia Ngu Street is Hang Be market, which has existed for nearly a hundred years. At number 50 there is an ancient communal house called Dai Loi. Over the years, Dai Loi has become a spiritual place for local people.

Turn right into Hang Dao Street.

HÀNG ĐÀO

PEACH STREET

This was historically one of the first streets in the Old Quarter. Hang Dao is a fruity name which translates to Peach street. In the Tran-Ho dynasty of the 14th - 15th century, the merchants sold silk, including a very special peach flower silk. In the 15th century, the tube house at number 38 sold peach flower silk and silk tunics for royal palace courtiers. Five centuries later you can buy natural silks and fabric here.

The architecture in Hang Dao, is from the French Colonial period of 1900-30 and the French Art Deco style of 1930-45. The building frontages are a mix of romantic oriental French and ancient tube houses.

Number 38 is a restored two story home, a spacious and elaborate example of a wealthy silk merchant's house. Number 39 is a piece of living history. A great example of an old French oriental villa, right down to its crumbling plaster facade. The restoration of this house has been completed thanks to collaboration between the French and Vietnamese. For more restoration information see www.toulouse.fr

Opening times 9-11am and in the afternoon from 2-5pm, Monday to Friday. You can buy replica maps of old Hanoi city as it was in 1873. They also serve traditional Vietnamese tea and will show you around the house, for a small fee.

Number 64 is a traditional tube house which has been restored to its original state. It also has a display in the courtyard featuring historical research; renovation details and information on various architectural styles found in the Old Quarter. There is an exhibition which features the original types of clay tiles, which give the buildings such a distinctive look throughout the city. Number 70 is a classic tube house with a traditional orange clay tiled roof.

Hang Dao turns into the Hang Dao Dong Xuan market, a famous night market on Friday, Saturday and Sunday evenings from 7pm. This around-the-clock night market runs the length of Hang Dao Street to the Dong Xuan Market.

Go straight onto Hang Ngan Street.

HÀNG NGANG

CROSS STREET

Hang Ngan Street is located in the old ward of Dien Hung. In the 18th century, Hang Ngan was known as Hang Lam Street where vendors specialized in selling a special blue silk used to make traditional Vietnamese dresses.

This street was (and still is) populated by two communities, Vietnamese and Chinese. The Vietnamese were the Minh Huong people and the Chinese were the people of Hau Le.

The Chinese Hau Le people formed Feudal courts in the late Le Dynasty which ruled the country from 1428 to 1788. The Le Emperors introduced the Chinese system of civil service. At this time massive changes took place in Vietnamese society. The Buddhist state became Confucian, based on Chinese principles. The Chinese instigated the laws.

The Minh Huong people were the spiritual brokers who brought together Chinese religious worship and the traditional worship of the Vietnamese. This is illustrated at the Tam Thanh Temple, where both forms of beliefs are being worshiped.

Hang Ngan was an exclusive area and only the rich traded there. It remains the busiest and most prosperous street in Hanoi. Number 7 and number 27 were homes of wealthy silk traders.

Number 48 is a historical shrine where Ho Chi Minh wrote the Vietnamese declaration of independence. This house is an historic revolutionary landmark.

Number 62 sells pearls from Phu Quoc Island (including highly sought after black pearls), precious stones and jade (known as the diamond of the North). The store also has an extensive collection of traditional gold and silver jewelry.

Turn right into Hang Buom Street.

HÀNG BUỒM

SAIL STREET

Hang Buom Street was near the Red River, before the river changed its course. Nautical equipment and sails were sold here, for the boats trading up and down the Red River.

In 500 AD Ly Nam De built a garrison in Hang Buom. He was deemed to be the first emperor of Vietnam by the people. For them he stood as a symbol of equal power, in their protest against the Chinese imperial rulers of the time. He successfully expelled the Liang administration and led the insurrection that ended in 543. In February 544, he was declared the official emperor of Vietnam.

The mythology of this street tells of the King and a white horse. The King wanted to build a citadel to establish a stable base of power in Hanoi. Yet, the project failed repeatedly. Hanoi was originally a swamp and not suitable for large citadel construction.

The King was praying at the Long Do temple in

Hang Buom Street, when a vision of a white horse appeared to him. The horse was circling around the failed construction site. Before disappearing into the sky, the horse left hoof prints in the mud. The King interpreted the vision as a good omen. He arranged for the citadel to be constructed within the mystical circle of the white horse's hoof prints. The construction was finally successful. The King honored the white mythical horse as the God of Thang Long (Hanoi).

Take time to wander the picturesque streets of this well-loved neighborhood. All along the street there are colonial buildings, traditional Vietnamese houses and song birds singing in bamboo cages.

Look out for rose sellers in the morning. Hanoi roses are beautifully perfumed. You will need to haggle a bit, but bunches are around 30,000-50,000 VND for pink musk or yellow roses. It is worth filling your hotel room with their heavenly perfume.

As well as a street of worship, the locals pay homage to their love of sweet things here. The local description of Hang Buom is now 'Candy and Alcohol Street'. There are plenty of snacks, alcohol and coffee, food stores, candy stores and stalls selling preserved tropical fruit; and nuts like locally grown pistachio and cashews.

If you are a self confessed foodie and want to learn how to cook traditional Vietnamese cooking, number 7 Hang Buom holds daily cooking classes.

Number 22 is a well preserved communal house. The shops at Number 28 and 31 are connoisseur tea-shops. You can buy traditional Vietnamese tea and boutique teas from around the world. This place is a delight. They sell a large range of delicate china cups and oriental tea pots. Number 34 is a factory outlet selling international brands of clothing and shoes such as Zara and Alda.

This street has a number of Mexican, Indian and Middle Eastern restaurants. Number 57 is a traditional wooden restaurant. Nice atmosphere with great value Vietnamese food. Number 62 sells collectible propaganda posters. Originals and prints. Light and easy gifts to roll up.

At number 76 Hang Buom, two old communal houses are still standing. Nearby is the famous Bach Ma temple built in A.D. 1010. A grand courtyard of massive red pillars, Buddhist statues and alters. Certified as a historical, religious site, this famous temple is dedicated to the earth spirit, the To Lich river spirit and his messenger, the sacred White Horse.

If you want to stock up on bling party shoes, boots, bags and sandals, open the shop door at number 83. Towards the end of the street are some traditional family run coffee houses. Vietnam produces billions of tons of coffee a year, making it the second highest producer in the world ranking, next to Brazil. Coffee is as much a part of the Vietnamese culture, as the conical hat. At number 103, the owners will brew you a taste of any kind of coffee you like, including the famous weasel coffee. They will tell you a wee tale about that. Try the Parisian beans roasted in butter. The recipe goes back to French colonial rule. Number 108 is a traditional restaurant selling delicious Vietnamese roasted duck and suckling pig.

So you've bought a few things. Don't worry, you can easily post them home by dropping into a post office and sending those extra parcels ahead. All you need is your passport and some local money.

Turn right into Hang Giay which runs into Luong Ngoc Quyen Street.

HANG GIẦY

Walking can get tiring, so this is a tiny green space, off the main drag, where you can take a break. This end of Hang Giay is shady and quiet. A few local cats peacefully asleep on chairs. At night, the locals come to drink, chat and enjoy the cooler evening air.

This street runs into Luong Ngoc Quyen.

LƯƠNG NGỌC QUYÊN

N amed after the scholar Luong Ngoc Quyen (1885-1917). Luong Ngoc Quyen and his brother were the first to respond to the call of the Dong Du movement, to rise up against the French colonial rule. In order to prepare for the uprising, he studied arms and military strategy in a Japanese military school, in 1905.

In late 1914 he was arrested by British police in Hong Kong. Later, he moved to France. The French government issued a life sentence and sent him back to Vietnam, where he was jailed in Thai Nguyên province. While in jail, he organized and recruited insurgents for an uprising against the French. Then, on the night of August, 30th, 1917, the uprising began. They fought for six days, taking control of the Thai Nguyen Province. The French counter attacked successfully and Luong Ngoc Quyen was killed by French fire.

Number 18 was The Dong Do Theatre, 1945-1954. Sadly the theatre is no longer open, but you can see remnants of the old movie posters on the building.

On the corner of Ta Hien and Luong Ngoc Quy-en there are three popular places to get a cold beer. This place is known as Bai Hoi Corner. Traditional beer is served in street side beer houses known as Bia Hoi. The beer, light in flavor, is served straight from the keg.

Turn left into Ta Hien Street.

TẠ HIỆN

The street is named after the military commander, Ta Quang Hien. A leader of the patriot movement against the French.

The architecture in Ta Hien Street is a blend of oriental and western architectural styles. Cobble stone streets, restaurants, bars, massage services and art galleries. Quiet in the day, but full of extra atmosphere at night with tourists and locals. This area had an illicit red light district in Sam Cong and Hai Tuong alleys. In the Quang Lac Alley, Hanoians used to watch a Geisha style of entertainment in the Tuong Opera house. This theatre is now called the Ta Hien Theatre.

Number 2B is a craft house. A family run traditional wood block carving business. The owner, Pham Tinh, will carve the stamps, while you wait. He and his wife have been designing stamps and carving here for fifty-six years.

Turn right at the end and continue on Hang Buom then turn right into Dao Duy Tu.

ĐÀO DUY TỪ

N amed after Dao Duy Tu, (1572-1634). The highest ranking mandarin of his time. A military man of culture, born into a family of the Tuong opera artists. Historically only wealthy merchants and intellectuals patronized the Tuong Opera, but it quickly gained popularity, after he introduced it to the royal courts.

Dao Duy Tu Street historically traded raw and processed rice. Examples of the rice trade can be seen in the architecture. The houses are two, three and four story buildings, with bays for storing and trading rice. Houses numbered from 6 - 14 retain French colonial architecture. Number 14 sells traditional Vietnamese tea and cakes made to a secret family recipe.

At the end of Dao Duy Tu turn left walk a few meters and turn right into Ma May.

MA MAY

RATTAN STREET

Merchants and shops in Ma May Street traditionally sold votive papers and palanquins for honoring ancestors. Hanoians still buy votives and palanquins there today.

Ma May is also known as Revolution Street. During the French revolution, all the tube houses along the street had secret access ways through the internal walls. The revolutionaries could traverse the length of the street, undetected by the colonialists. The restaurant at number 69 has a bricked over revolutionary door, behind the bar. This bar/restaurant retains the old traditional style of architecture and has a traditional Vietnamese food menu.

Number 64 is the Huong Tuong Temple which dates from 1450 AD. There is an official stele in the temple which establishes that the temple was built in the Tran Dynasty.

Number 87 is one of the most interesting architectural sights in the city; a refurbished and restored traditional two-storied wooden house. Open every day for visitors, this home offers a unique opportunity to step back in time to have a close look at the interior of a traditional Old Quarter home. According to ancient Feng Sui rules, the back of the house is wider than the front; to bring the owners happiness and wealth. There are three distinct divisions in the house. House one: The ground floor of house one is a shop, the upper floor is for guest reception and houses the family alter. House two: the ground floor is the servants' quarters and a warehouse for storage. The upper floor is a bedroom with a front veranda where the owners could sit drinking tea and play chess. A rear veranda overlooks an open yard where Chinese medicinal herbs were dried. House three: a warehouse. This residence is typical of retail houses in the 19th century.

Turn right into Hang Mam Street to follow the walk on this map. However, if you wish to detour to see the funeral shops, turn left and walk a few meters up Hang Mam. Then come back and continue to Hang Bac Street.

HÀNG MAM

FISH SAUCE STREET

Nuoc Mam or fish sauce is a staple ingredient in Vietnamese cooking. Up to thirty years ago, shrimp sauce was sold here, presented in earthen pots, jars and barrels.

Hang Mam now makes tombstones and coffins. Locals call it 'Coffin Street'. Number 24 - 28 make traditional head stones and bone containers in the form of pots and porcelain boxes. This is where the Vietnamese arrange funeral activities, so sensitivity on the part of the tourist to respect this area is appreciated.

Hang Mam turns into Hang Bac Street.

HÀNG BẠC

SILVER STREET

Hang Bac is one of the oldest and most popular streets in the Old Quarter, dating from the 13th century. During the French colonial period, Hang Bac Street was named Rue Des Changeurs (city of money-changers).

Hang Bac has always honored the silversmith guild, but the street now has jewelry shops selling gold, silver and gemstones. At the time of writing there were eighty-two jewelry shops here.

Number 42 is a communal house honoring the ancestors of silver smiths, dating back to the 16th century. In the 16th century number 58 was a forge for casting silver coins and bullion for the royal court. Today it is still a temple of worship, but it also presents traditional musical performances called Ca Tru. This style of musical performance dates back to the time of the ancient royal courts. If you wish to know more refer to the web site at www.catru.com.vn

The next street is Dinh Liet. When you see the Dinh Liet Street sign, turn right into Dinh Liet, then twenty meters down, turn left into Ngo Trung Yen.

ĐINH LIỆT

KNITTING STREET

Historically this has been the one stop street for haberdashery. There are still knitting shops for wool, needles, knitted sweaters and scarves. Dinh Liet also has boutique shops specializing in beads, jewelry, silk scarves and bags.

7A Quan Bia Minh is a popular restaurant with expats. Upstairs in the old French colonial house there is a shady veranda and a view of the street. Number 4B has a photo gallery with well-observed artistic photos of Vietnam.

Turn left into Ngo Trung Yen: a small lane.

NGÕ TRUNG YÊN

S hady trees and songbirds. It's a magical place to walk down. A small village feel with locals sitting in doorways, talking with neighbors and friends. Local street markets with women selling fresh vegetables and tropical fruit. Market activities happen in the early morning and the cool climes of late afternoon.

At the end of this lane is Ngo Cau Co. A busy flower market in the morning. Late afternoon, a fresh meat and poultry market.

After Ngo Trung Yen turn left into Gia Ngu Street and turn right into Hang Be Street.

HÀNG BÈ

BAMBOO RAFT STREET

B amboo Raft Street was adjacent to the Red River before the river changed its course. Hundreds of rafts floated down river each day carrying forest bamboo for construction and unloading it in Hang Be Street. Bamboo, rattan goods and dried beetle nuts were sold here.

All these items are still sold here, especially betal nut and betal leaf. Both are important symbols of love and marriage for the Vietnamese.

For the famous charcoal grilled Bun Cha look for a little alley called Ngo Phat Loc. Number 42 sells silks, souvenirs and traditional handicrafts. Number 48 is The Green Tangerine restaurant. This restaurant, in a 1928 French colonial building, has an exotic east west menu and an inviting shady courtyard.

Walk straight on, as Hang Be Street runs directly into Hang Dau Street.

HÀNG DẦU

This is a bustling shoe street; selling every brand of shoe you can imagine. Shoes are made in Vietnam for export to all the major cities in the world. From Brazilian flip-flops to Nike's and hiking boots. Every shop in this street sells shoes and once you find your size and style, you can bargain around.

Sim cards and mobile phones are sold at number 26, on the corner of Hang Dau Street.

Turn right into Lo Su Street.

LÒ SŨ

PORCELAIN STREET

Lo Su Street once specialized in porcelain vases, incense holders and porcelain figurines for the worship of ancestors. Originally the porcelain craft serviced the Thang Long (Hanoi) Citadel. Today, porcelain is made in villages; leaving only the name. Now there are bag shops here. Travel bags are well priced in Hanoi, especially if you are prepared to bargain.

Notice the large old tree, still standing here from ancient times. Locals worship the tree's nature spirits and daily offerings are placed in the tree. At the end of the street turn right and you are back at The Water Puppet Theatre. If you have time to see the Ngoc Son Temple, go across the road. Walk over the famous red bridge to finish your walk right there in the middle of the jade green Hoan Kiem Lake.

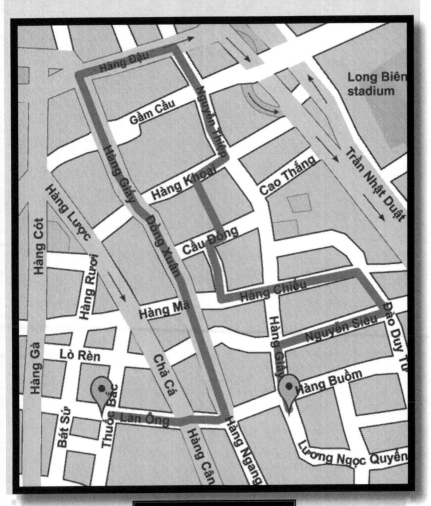

TRADITIONAL MEDICINE WALK

DISTANCE: 2 KILOMETERS. TIME: APPROX 2 HOUR WALK.

LÃN ÔNG

Lan Ong is named after a learned Mandarin scholar who wrote sixty-three traditional oriental medicine books. Lan Ong is still home to ethnic Chinese who sell herbs and medicine. The buildings date back to the 17th century. Look for tile roofs covered in moss, as these are the original homes of the Chinese.

Pungent earthy aromas fill the street. The shops sell herbs, teas, roots and dried fruits. Here illnesses and ailments are diagnosed by natural medicine doctors trained in traditional medicine diagnosis and healing methods. Prescribed herbs are selected from small drawers on massive dark wood cabinets or from glass apothecary jars, weighed and measured; then wrapped in paper packages and tied with twine. Verbal instructions are given on how to prepare a tea or infusion with the herbs, bark, seeds and fungi.

Aside from medicinal healing, there are herbs

for special teas to promote health and longevity, increase stamina, prevent flu and colds, keep eyes bright, skin clear and promote beauty. From the bitter artichoke root tea served everywhere on the street, to the fragrant lotus, perfumed jasmine to chrysanthemum blossom tea. Tea is an important part of the Vietnamese culture.

Today there are fifty-one traditional medicine outlets. Many of the shops have had the tradition of selling oriental medicinal herbs past down through the generations.

Pharmacies selling western pharmaceutical drugs: migraine, heart medication, ointments, steroid creams, anti-depressants and Viagra are sold on request, without prescription. For tourists in the medical profession, it's a jaw-dropping experience seeing what is sold on the streets.

Turn left into Hang Ngang Street.

HÀNG NGANG

Hang Ngan Street is located in the old ward of Dien Hung. In the 18th century, Hang Ngan was known as Hang Lam Street where vendors specialized in selling a special blue silk used to make traditional Vietnamese dresses.

This street was (and still is) populated by Vietnamese and Chinese. The Vietnamese are the Minh Huong people and the Chinese are the people of Hau Le. The Chinese Hau Le people formed feudal courts in the late Le Dynasty which ruled the country from 1428 to 1788. The Le emperors introduced the Chinese system of civil service. At this time massive change took place in Vietnamese society. The Buddhist state became Confucian, based on Chinese principles. The Chinese instigated the laws.

The Minh Huong people were the spiritual brokers who brought together Chinese religious worship and the traditional worship of the Vietnamese. This is illustrated at the Tam Thanh Temple, where both forms of beliefs are being worshiped.

Hang Ngan was an exclusive area and only the rich traded there. It remains the busiest and most prosperous street in Hanoi. Number 7 and number 27 were homes of wealthy silk traders.

Number 48 is a historical shrine where Ho Chi Minh wrote the Vietnamese declaration of independence. This house is an historic revolutionary landmark.

Number 62 sells pearls from Phu Quoc Island (including highly sought after black pearls), precious stones and jade (known as the diamond of the North). The store also has an extensive collection of traditional gold and silver jewelry.

Carry straight on into Dong Xuan Street.

DONG XUAN

Dong Xuan Street is famous for the Dong Xuan market. Located in the heart of the Old Quarter. On the night of July 14th, 1994, a fire engulfed the entire market, causing three hundred billion Vietnamese dongs worth of damage. The market has been rebuilt, but modeled on the previous architecture.

Dong Xuan is mostly a wholesale market and distribution point for retailers, in Hanoi. Suppliers mainly come from North Vietnam. The market has an extensive range of electronic devices, household equipment and clothing. Inside the market, towards the back, animals (puppies, kittens, birds and fish) are bought and sold for pets. Vietnamese bonsai trees are sold here. The bonsai trees are native tropical species in miniature, these include guava, plum, mango, lemon, rose and more. Markets are all about bargaining for the best buy. Vendors argue the price with each other; there's an urban saying that, "Two women and a duck make a market". The northern end of the market, is the food market, where local women prepare and serve fresh Vietnamese food all day.

Walk straight along Dong Xuan towards Hang Giay Street.

HÀNG GIẤY

PAPER STREET

This was the first street to make and sell paper. The French colonials named it Rue Du Papier. After the Revolution, the street name reverted to its original Vietnamese name, Hang Giay. Today you can buy local handmade and imported paper here. This is a popular street for street food restaurants serving traditional bun (noodle) meals. Bun is served for breakfast lunch and dinner. This famous noodle dish is as varied as the fresh seasonal ingredients of snail, quail eggs, frogs, beef, shrimp, chicken and tofu.

During the day, Hanoians like to sit beside small stalls on the street drinking their favorite che drink.

Che consists of tropical fruit, crushed ice, sweet tapioca balls, jelly squares and coconut milk.

Hang Giay is also famous for small street side restaurants which sell salads of dried beef jerky, fresh herbs, shredded carrot and a spicy dressing.

Turn right into Hang Dau Street.

HÀNG DẦU

OIL STREET

Once, Hang Dau Street merchants sold oil; betel oil, cooking oils, artists oil and oil for lamps. Now it is a one-stop destination for export quality shoes, trainers, boots and flipflops, for the European markets. Over-runs, samples and surplus stock fill the shops here.

Turn right into Nguyen Thiep Street.

NGUYỄN THIỆP

Number 27, is an ancient temple built in 1690. The structure was damaged during the Vietnam war and has since been restored. Today, the temple is a landmark building which houses historical pieces, such as the ancient stele of the temple. Turn right into Hang Khoai Street.

HÀNG KHOAI

POTATO STREET

Yes, you guessed it. The dirt on this street is that vendors sold potatoes, taro and root vegetables. You won't find taro now, but at number 6 there is an ancient Taoist temple. In the temple there is a stele plaque dating the temple's registration, as 1668 AD.

Local shops sell traditional goods for everyday use; bamboo baskets, rope, incense, glazed porcelain cups, bowls, plates, vases, statues, jars, clay pots and ceramic funeral urns.

Next turn left and go into Ngo Hang Chieu and then cross Cua Dong Street and continue down Ngo Hang Chieu then turn left into Hang Chieu Street.

HÀNG CHIẾU

MAT STREET

In the past, sedge mats were sold here. In 1872, a merchant named Jean Dupuis befriended the locals in this street. However, he was actually a spy for the French colonialist government. Due to his information, the French military were able to enter Hanoi, along Hang Chieu road, surprising and defeating the local Vietnamese strong hold.

Keeping up with the 21st century, vendors here sell plastic floor mats as well as traditional sedge mats.

Turn right into Dao Duy Tu Street.

ĐÀO DUY TỪ

Named after Dao Duy Tu (1572-1634), who was the highest ranking mandarin of his time. A military man of culture, born into a family of the Tuong opera artists. The Tuong Opera gained further popularity after he introduced it to the royal courts. Previously only wealthy merchants and intellectuals patronized the Tuong Opera.

Dao Duy Tu Street historically traded raw and processed rice. Examples of rice trade are seen in the architecture. The houses are two, three and four story buildings, with bays for storing and trading rice. The houses numbered from 6 - 14 retain French colonial architecture. Number 14 sells traditional Vietnamese tea and cakes made to a secret family recipe.

Turn right into Nguyen Van Sieu Street.

NGUYỄN SIÊU

Named after a noted 18th century Mandarin scholar and Confucian master. He was a poet and historian who wrote literature on history, geography and philosophy. A poetic genius, he was praised for being a God of poetry by his contemporaries.

Number 28 is a communal house located in the alley. Students stayed here when they attended Sieu's lectures.

The temple in Nguyen Van Sieu is over a hundred years old. It is dedicated to women saints such as Lieu Hanh and Princess Bach Hoa. Inside there is a bell, ancient parallel verses and objects used for worship of their cult.

Turn left into Hang Giay. Walk down and cross over Hang Buom Street. This part of the street is the end of Hang Giay Street. A leafy, shady street, as it turns into the beginning of Luong Ngoc Quyen.

HANG GIẦY

This end of Hang Giay is shady and quiet. A few local cats peacefully asleep on chairs. At night, the locals come to drink, chat and enjoy the cooler evening air.

This street is the final old quarter street of the Traditional Medicine Street City Walk.

THE SECRET CAFÉ WALK

DISTANCE: 3km. TIME: APPROX 2-4 HOUR WALK.

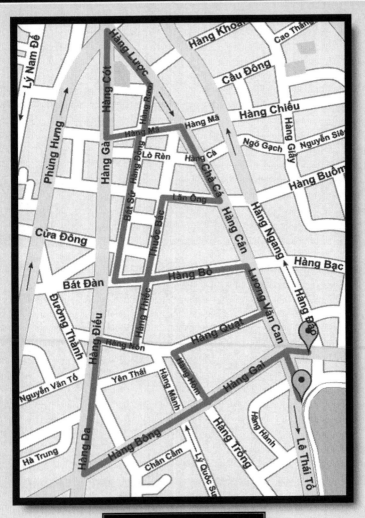

LƯƠNG VĂN CAN

S tart at the Thuy Ta café at number 1 Le Thai To Street, which is beside the ancient mystical Hoan Kiem Lake. Walk directly across Le Thai To Street, turn right and walk up Luong Van Can Street. The beginning of this street just sells sunglasses, reading glasses and prescription glasses. Vietnamese don't pay import duty. So genuine fashion brands can be a third of the cost. Check the quality of the sunglasses, by asking the store owner to test the UV factor of the lenses. Lenses in the 350 to 400 range meet international standards for UV protection.

Turn left into Hang Gai Street.

HÀNG GAI

HEMP STREET

n the 15th century, Hang Gai Street sold rope and jute products. From the 19th century, print workshops made wood block prints and books were sold here.

Hang Gai now has boutique shops and galleries. This street is now the best street to buy silk and high quality linen products. Most shops here sell bedding and clothing; traditional wedding quilts, hand embroidered bed sheets, tablecloths, cushions, hand smocked baby dresses, dinner napkins and duvet cover sets. Professional dressmakers and men's tailors offer a walk in service. Number 66 Tan My, has a three generation silk and embroidery tradition. All embroidery is done by hand. Number 61 Tan My Design, is opposite the original Tan My shop. Three retail floors highlight Vietnamese designer clothing fashion, accessories and homeware. Khai Silk at Number 96 and 113 is the largest retail silk stockist in Hanoi.

Number 41, Thang Long Art Gallery, sells contemporary Vietnamese art. Number 46 is a communal house worshiping Qui Minh, a brother of Son Tinh, the legendary mountain god who fought Thuy Tinh, the god of the sea. This is now a private house with no religious items, but you can see two small stone lion-dogs on the arched entrance, on the To Tich side of the building. Number 83 was the residence of the first French minister in Hanoi.

Hang Gai used to be part of the Co Vu village and their communal house was founded at number 85, honoring Bach Ma and Ling Lang. The hundred year old banyan tree, in front of number 83, is revered as a small temple. Burning incense and offerings of local rice wine are placed daily in the alcoves and at the base of the tree.

Turn right into Hang Hom Street.

HÀNG HÒM

Wood craftsmen set up shop in Hang Hom Street in the 19th century. They produced black stained wooden trunks for clothing and multi-drawer chests for paper storage. They engraved wooden alter panels and made small boxes for holding betel leaves and areca nuts. Later, the woodworks were decorated with lacquer, using the resin of the special tree, rhus succedanea. Lacquerware became popular for bowls, trays and furniture.

In the 1930's, Vietnamese artists, in collaboration with French artists, developed a distinct genre of fine art lacquer painting, sometimes applying more than ten layers or more of black, red, brown or clear lacquer. Today the tradition of lacquer art is still a commercial and cultural activity in Hang Hom. The Communal House at number 11 was constructed for worshiping Tra Lu, the ancestor of lacquer painting.

People from the original village still worship there.

Fierce battles were fought with the French in this street in 1947 and 1954.

Turn right into Hang Quat Street.

HÀNG QUẠT

FAN STREET

Hang Quat Street traditionally sold silk and paper fans made by the villagers in Dao Xa (Top Fan). In the French colonial period, it was called "rue des Eventails" (Hanging fans).

Today Hang Quat sells ceremonial clothing, wedding items, decorations for ancestral shrines, prayer flags and wood blocks for printing prayer papers. This is an important street for local people.

The daily ceremony of ancestor worship is performed in every home and shop. Shrines are decorated with golden statues, jewels, candles, incense, alcohol, fruits, food, cigarettes and other worldly offerings, for the family ancestors.

Number 4 is a communal house honoring the

founder of fan making. It is also a memorial honoring the patriotic martyrs who died in battles and prisons during the French colonial period.

Number 43 was the first private school for continuing education. Number 64 is a popular temple for worship; The Dau temple, dedicated to the Mother Saint of Hanoi, Lieu Hanh.

At the end of Hang Quat Street, hats, lutes and religious objects were made. Today, hats, traditional costumes and embroidered dresses are sold here.

Turn left into Luong Van Can Street.

LUONG VAN CAN

The street is named after Luong Van Can (1854-1927). He was a Vietnamese mandarin, school administrator, independence activist and writer. He was a propagandist and patriotic agitator against the French colonial rule. His most noted work is Nha Nuoc, 'The State'. In 1907, he was co- founder of the famous Dong Kinh Nghia Thuc (Tonkin Free School). The school printed many books calling for innovative policies and new ways of thinking to enhance the education and intelligence of the people. He was arrested by the French and exiled to Con Dao Island. He died on June 12, 1927 at number 4 Hang Dao Street.

The houses from number 6 - 18 were used as the first Tuong Opera Theatre in Hanoi. Now known as The Thang Long Music and Dance Theatre.

Shops in this street sell children's games and toys that will satisfy every child's dream.

Traditional women's dress called Ao Dai can be bought at number 6 and number 8. These stores specialize in Ao Dai design which are long dresses, with petite mandarin collars, two slits up the side and worn over flowing silk pants.

The shop owners in this street migrated from the village called Truch Xa. Consequently most of the shop names include the word Truch, for example, An Truch, Phuc Truch, Binh Truch, Hung Truch. This is the way local people still keep close ties to their villages.

Turn left into Hang Bo Street.

HÀNG BÒ

BAMBOO BASKET STREET

Hang Bo had small traditional houses where bamboo baskets, clogs and sandals were sold. Now Hang Bo sells needles, thread, beads, buttons, zippers and clippers. There is a French bakery and cake shop at number 20.

In the evening, all vendor stalls disappear and mats are thrown down on the footpaths. This is a popular street where the Vietnamese meet friends to talk, eat barbecued cuttlefish, and drink beer.

Turn right into Thuoc Bac Street.

THUỐC BẮC

For a decade, traditional Chinese and Vietnamese medicinal herbs were sold here. Later, the herb shops moved to Lang Ong.

The street was originally called Hang Lock Street. During the French colonial period, the market sold iron products; iron pipes, iron sheets and locks. As you walk north today, artisans solder, hammer and beat metal pieces right on the pavement. Retail shops here sell imported metal goods; tools, safes, pots, locks and mirrors.

Turn right into Lan Ong Street.

LÃN ÔNG

TRADITIONAL MEDICINE STREET

Lan Ong is named after a learned mandarin scholar who wrote sixty-three traditional oriental medicine books.

Pungent earthy aromas fill the street. The shops sell herbs, teas, roots and dried fruits. Here illnesses and ailments are diagnosed by natural medicine doctors trained in traditional medicine diagnosis and healing methods. Prescribed herbs are selected from small wooden drawers or glass jars, weighed and measured; then wrapped in paper packages and tied with twine. Verbal instructions are given on how to prepare a tea or infusion with the herbs, bark, seeds and fungi, at home. Aside from medicinal healing, there are special herb teas with specific properties to promote health, longevity, increase stamina, prevent flu's and colds and promote beauty.

Tea is an important ceremony and part of the Vietnamese culture. From the bitter artichoke root tea, to the fragrant lotus and chrysanthemum teas blooming in china cups.

Today there are fifty-one traditional medicine outlets. Many of the shops have had the tradition of selling oriental medicinal herbs passed down through the generations. Shops around here also sell vitamins and quality skin care products: pharmaceutical drugs for migraine, heart medication, ointments, steroid creams, anti-depressants and Viagra are sold on request, without prescription. For tourists in the medical profession, it's a jaw-dropping experience seeing what is sold on the streets.

Turn left into Cha Ca Street.

CHẢ CÁ

GRILLED FISH STREET

I n 1885 the Doan family, opened a restaurant at number 14 Hang Son Street called 'Cha Ca La Vong'. The restaurant featured a signature dish of butter-coated barbecued fish cooked at the table with dill, turmeric and spring onions with peanuts, vermicelli noodles, secret sauce and leafy herb salad on the side. The dish was so well appreciated by the local Hanoi people, they named the street after the fish dish. The restaurant at number 14 has been serving their famous grilled fish dishes for over one hundred years. Note the old wooden staircase and family antiques. In the restaurant, there's a statue of La Vong, an old fisherman, with a rod in one hand and a fishing line dangling in the other.

Turn left into Hang Ma Street.

HÀNG MÃ

JOSS PAPER STREET

Today locals buy incense, religious votives and traditional funeral maps for their ancestor worshipping in Hang Ma.

Marriage invitations, business cards and flyers are designed and printed in shops all along this street. The selection of paper and card is varied. Quality standards are high. Check their samples.

Sheets of paper; plain, colored, art paper, striped, dotted, imported or handmade, can be purchased on Hang Ma. Also known as 'Lantern Street'; selling traditional Hoi Anh style lanterns, wood and paper lamps, outdoor lanterns and the silk lotus shaped lamps that are synonymous with Vietnam.

Turn right into Hang Ruoi Street.

HÀNG RƯƠI

This street owes its name to one of five hundred saltwater worm species. People from coastal towns came up the river once a year, in sandworm season, to sell sandworms in Hang Ruoi. Now the Red River has receded, the port has gone, but every year, in sandworm season, sellers call out "Does anyone want to buy my sandworms?"

Sandworms, although the name sounds a dash unappetizing, are considered to be a rare delicacy. The sandworms (nereidae) sold here, are grilled, stewed or made into sauce for Vietnamese dishes.

Go left up Hang Luoc Street.

HÀNG LƯỢC

COMB STREET

The long, black lustrous hair of the Vietnamese women is iconic. So you can understand how a whole street could have once been dedicated to hair combs.

Hang Luoc Street is now known as Flower Street, by the locals. On December 23rd (lunar calendar year) until new years eve and leading up to the Tet celebrations, kumquat trees, apricot and peach blossom trees line the streets and fill the markets. If you are in Hanoi at this time, be sure to visit the floral market here at Hang Luoc. You'll see thousands of birds of paradise flowers, gorgeous French roses in bloom and sacred lotus flowers. The air is filled with damask rose perfume. Flowers and blossom trees are delivered into Hanoi from as far away as Ho Chi Minh and Dalat. Visiting the flower market in Hang Luoc is a long standing cultural tradition in Hanoi.

Turn left into Hang Cot Street.

HÀNG CÓT

Hang Cot and Hang Ga are part of an ancient road that led to and from Hanoi. Many bamboo craftsmen set up shops on these streets. Traditionally bamboo was the building material used for lattice screens, scaffolding, buildings, decorative objects for the home; tables, chairs, curtain rails, ladders and drinking cups.

Today in Hang Cot Street, bamboo ladders and bamboo poles tower above the street, outside the stores. At number 44, in Hang Cot pagoda, an intriguing set of wooden Buddhist scripts can be seen. Number 54 is an ancient communal house, dedicated to the lattice makers deity.

Turn left into Hang Ma, then right into Hang Dong

HÀNG ĐỒNG

COPPER STREET

In Hang Dong Street, traditional craftsmen made copper platters, casseroles, pots and pans for the royal courts. Later artisans improved their skills and made complex products such as antique trays, bird statues, incense burners, candle holders and singing bowls.

Today workshops make similar traditional objects and iron balustrades, handrails, copper sign boards and doors. A number of shops sell the famous Phuc Loc Tho porcelain.

Go straight on into Bat Su Street.

BÁT SỰ

CERAMIC BOWL STREET

B at Su was one of the original thirty-six streets of the Old Quarter. Craftsmen made pottery, ceramics and porcelain. Today traditional porcelain and ceramics are still sold in Bat Su Street. Number 52 is Bat Su's preserved traditional communal house, characterized by its low, tiled roof line. The house is used for worshiping ancestors of the ceramic village, it's located on the corner of Bat Su and Cua Dong Streets.

There is a cozy local cafe on the corner of this busy street.

Turn left into Bat Dan Street.

BÁT ĐÀN

PORCELAIN BOWL STREET

I n the early 20th century, even numbered houses sold clay bowls that were brought to the city from riverside workshops on the Red River. Odd numbers sold leather and wood items.

Drop into number 49 Bat Dan Street for a bowl of the famous Hanoi pho (soup). This restaurant uses a much prized secret family recipe. Number 33 is an ornate communal house.

Turn left into Hang Bo Street, then right into Hang Thiec Street.

HÀNG THIẾC

TIN STREET

H ang Thiec was originally a village called Yen Noi. Before the French colonial period, the village produced religious items in cast pewter; lamps, candle holders, incense burners, kettles, cups and engraved pewter trays. Antique pewter can be found here. Metal products in brass, copper, iron and stainless steel are crafted on the pavement. The southern end of the street sells hammers, bolt cutters, screwdrivers, screws, nails, bolts, blades and scissors.

Most houses here are built in the ancient matchbox style; beams made from ironwood and small mezzanine galleries. The lower floors are prone to flooding, during monsoon season.

Turn right into Hang Non Street.

HÀNG NÓN

CONICAL HAT STREET

Traditional conical hats for men were made from pineapple leaves or feathers with a silver or copper knob at the top. Noble women wore wide flat palm leaf hats with fringes called Nghe. On labor sites today, workers wear conical hats, known as the Non La (leaf hat). The hat has become an iconic symbol. They are extremely versatile. Primarily used as protection from the sun and rain. When dipped in water, it becomes an evaporative cooling device. It is used as a basin to carry water or rice; a fan for a ploughman on a hot summer's day; a basket to carry a bunch of vegetables from the market, and for romantic couples to hide behind to steal a kiss. Today, you can still buy conical hats here and wooden clogs made in the Hang Hom village.

In 1928-29 the Youth Revolution Comrade Association met in a tobacco shop at Number 15.

Turn left into Hang Dieu Street.

HÀNG ĐIẾU

TOBACCO AND PIPE STREET

This street was once known as The Fire Place, due to the number of fires recorded in this area. In the 18th century, the fire problem was so bad, the government banned fire lighting at night; including lamps, pipes, cigarettes and water-pipe smoking. The fire ban was a problem for shop keepers, as Hang Dieu was a street full of tobacco shops. In The Spirit Fire Temple at number 30, a warning bell was hung. When a fire was ablaze, the bell was rung, alerting the locals.

The oldest profession in the world, carried on in the evenings at Number 76 and 82. Later the street diversified into leather goods; saddles, shoes and leather furniture were produced in the houses. The backyards had lime pools for curing hides.

Today shops sell leather shoes, cotton blankets, mattresses, pillows, bedding, jasmine tea and lotus jam. Lotus seed jam is a speciality of Hanoi. Drinking jasmine tea, while enjoying a plate of lotus seed jam, is to experience the taste of the real Hanoi.

Hang Dieu has speciality eel restaurants, popular with the locals. The eels are small and come from the surrounding cane fields on the outskirts of Hanoi. Fresh herb salads are served with crunchy fried strips of eel and spicy chili dressing, or soup and vermicelli with crispy eel.

Number 66 and 77 have historic architectual merit, with ornate filigree colonial edifices of a time when Hanoi was described as the Paris of the east.

Go straight on, as Hang Dieu Street runs into Hang Da Street.

HÀNG DA

This was once known as Fortune Tellers Street. The fortune tellers would sit outside Tan Thanh temple at number 40 and offer to tell worshipers their fortunes. Now the locals call number 40, the voodoo house.

During the Nguyen dynasty 1802-1945, Hang Da market sold fresh produce and live cattle. The inhabitants processed buffalo and ox hides, then tanned the hides and made bags and shoes.

Today, local craftsmen sell custom-made leather goods. Bags, belts and brief cases in buttery soft leather. Plus exotic leather products made from crocodile, ostrich and snake skin.

Turn left into Hang Bong Street.

HÀNG BÔNG

COTTON STREET

I n the 17th-18th century, Tay Son Trinh Lords bought gifts for the king in Hang Bong Street. Hang Bong Street is unusual, because it crosses a few ancient villages. When you walk down Hang Bong Street, the lanes to the left or right take you into the original village streets.

The villages of Hang Bong traded in fine cotton, blankets, cushions and pillows. Workshops for cotton production have now turned into retail shops selling fashion clothing, embroidered sheets, smocked dresses, finely embroidered table napkins, tablecloths and quilts made by women in the embroidery villages.

Bolts of cotton cloth are imported from China, Italy and Ireland, then hand embroidered in Vietnam. To determine quality, ask the shop-keeper about the origins of the fabric.

Hang Bong Street runs înto Hang Gai Street. Hang Gai has a hidden café at number 11. Make your way through a souvenir shop to the back and you enter an ancient interior court yard. This is a combined family house and a cafe. A place to soak up the atmosphere of a time gone by. Up on the top level (past the family alter room filled with antiques), you get a spectacular view of Hoan Kiem Lake. This hidden local cafe is a perfect place to finish this walk.

MAGICAL TURTLE WALK

DISTANCE: 2.5 KILOMETERS. TIME: APPROX 2-3 HOUR WALK.

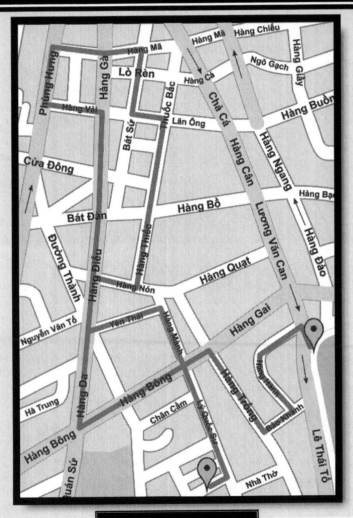

This walk starts at the Thuy Ta café at number 1 Le Thai To Street beside the lake. Before starting the walk, take a look into the waters of this legendary lake. There is a reason for this. If you see bubbles rising to the surface, take it as a sign that the ancient golden turtle of Hoan Kiem Lake is about to appear. If you see the ancient turtle of the Hoan Kiem Lake, it is a rare and fortunate occasion that brings good luck to those who see it. An opportunity to make a wish of a lifetime.

The second day we arrived in Hanoi, we saw a large golden turtle raise its head out of the water. We didn't know this legend, as we watched the golden turtle rise for air. Five times the turtle surfaced and not once did we know to make a wish! We missed five lifetime wishes each. Ten wishes total! So keep your eyes open! After hopefully seeing the turtle, turn around and go cross the road to where sunglasses are sold and turn right into Luong Van Can Street.

LƯƠNG VĂN CAN

SUNGLASSES STREET

The beginning of this street just sells sunglasses, reading glasses and prescription glasses. Vietnamese don't pay import duty. Genuine fashion brands are a third of the cost you would pay in other countries. Check the quality of the sunglasses, by asking the store owner to test the UV factor of the lenses. Lenses in the 350 to 400 range meet international standards for UV protection.

Turn left into Hang Hanh Street.

HÀNG HÀNH

A nice walking lane, close to the lake with Vietnamese coffee houses. Look for an upstairs cafe balcony for a vantage point to look at life going on in the street below. This characterful lane has bars, cafes, an authentic French bakery, pizzas, DVD shops, boutique hotels and travel agents. Number 11b The Apple Tart French bakery, makes the best citron lemon tart we have tasted. Handmade chocolate covered candied orange rind, pear and almond tarts and French bread are also delicious. Silk shops in this street have some gorgeous hand embroidered clothes, silk scarves, cashmere shawls and soft furnishings.

Turn right into Bao Khanh Street.

BẢO KHÀNH

During lunch time and evenings, in the street there is a Banh Cuon restaurant that serves thin rice pancakes with a choice of fillings. Cooked right in front of you, the pancakes make a delicious snack. You'll find several western style restaurants in this area.

Turn right into Hang Trong Street.

HÀNG TRỐNG

This street was part of the dike for the Red river. Many small villages set up here to make drums, parasols, awnings and canopies.

Many art galleries here today exhibit work by local artists. You will also see artists at work in the shops, copying works of the great masters and Impressionists. There is a heady smell of oil paint coming from shop doorways, as local artists are busy working on their canvases.

There are two ancient temples here. The first one at number 82 is dedicated to a talented singer. She had a successful singing career and used her earnings to support the poor. The narrow temple at number 82 is built directly over her tomb. The second temple (upstairs at number 75) is Huong temple. Dedicated to the four directional gods of Hanoi city: Tran Vu, Bach Ma, Linh Lang and Cao Son.

At the end of Hang Trong Street turn left into Hang Bong Street

HÀNG BÔNG

COTTON STREET

I n the 17th-18th century, Tay Son Trinh Lords bought gifts for the king in Hang Bong Street. Hang Bong Street is unusual because it crosses a few ancient villages. When you walk down Hang Bong Street, the lanes to the left or right take you into the original village streets.

The villages of Hang Bong traded in fine cotton, blankets, cushions and pillows. Workshops for cotton production have turned into retail shops selling fashion clothing, embroidered sheets, smocked dresses, finely embroidered table napkins, tablecloths and quilts made by women in the embroidery villages.

Bolts of cotton cloth are imported from China, Italy and Ireland, then hand embroidered in Vietnam. To determine quality, ask the shop-keeper about the origins of the fabric.

Turn right into Hang Manh Street.

HÀNG MÀNH

BAMBOO BLIND STREET

Over a hundred years ago, craftsmen from the Te Yen Phong district, brought bamboo blind making and cork floor manufacturing to Hang Manh Street. Today, four families follow the ancestral craft, making blinds for doors and windows. Hang Manh Street in the 1920's and 1930's was home to several infamous licensed brothels. In 1938, at the height of the resistance against the French colonists, the house at Number 1 was the secret base of the resistance group called Hoang Van Thu.

Turn left into Yen Thai Street.

YÊN THÁI

Ngo Yen Thai is one street that escaped the French colonial modernization plan for making the streets wider; turning alleys into streets and streets into boulevards. This street is still the width of a rickshaw. Yen Thai Street was home to rickshaw pullers, itinerant workers, carpenters and bricklayers. The women and children worked in the nearby Hang Da market.

Turn right into Hang Dieu Street.

HÀNG ĐIẾU

TOBACCO AND PIPE STREET

This street was once known as The Fire Place, due to the number of fires recorded in this area. In the 18th century, the fire problem was so bad, the government banned fire lighting at night; including lamps, pipes, cigarettes and water-pipe smoking. The fire ban was a problem for shop keepers, as Hang Dieu was a street full of tobacco shops. In The Spirit Fire Temple at number 30, a warning bell was hung. When a fire was ablaze, the bell was rung, alerting the locals.

The oldest profession in the world, carried on in the evenings at Number 76 and 82. Later the street diversified into leather goods; saddles, shoes and leather furniture were produced in the houses. The backyards had lime pools for curing hides.

Today shops sell leather shoes, cotton blankets, mattresses, pillows, bedding, jasmine tea and lotus jam. Lotus seed jam is a speciality of Hanoi. Drinking jasmine tea, while enjoying a plate of lotus seed jam, is to experience the taste of the real Hanoi.

Hang Dieu has speciality eel restaurants, popular with the locals. Fresh herb salads are served with crunchy fried strips of eel and spicy chili dressing, or soup and vermicelli with crispy eel.

Number 66 and 77 have historic architectual merit, with ornate filigree colonial edifices of a time when Hanoi was described as the Paris of the east.

Turn right into Hang Non Street.

HÀNG NÓN

CONICAL HAT STREET

Traditional conical hats for men were made from pineapple leaves or feathers with a silver or copper knob at the top. Noble women wore wide flat palm leaf hats with fringes called Nghe. The rural people wore hats that looked like flat baskets. In the 1920's only the poor workers engaged in heavy labor, wore conical hats.

On labor sites today, workers wear conical hats, known as the Non La (leaf hat). The hat has become an iconic symbol. They are extremely versatile. Primarily used as protection from the sun and rain. When dipped in water, it becomes an evaporative cooling device. It is used as a basin to carry water or rice; a fan for a ploughman on a hot summer's day; a basket to carry a bunch of vegetables from the market, and for romantic couples to hide behind to steal a kiss.

Today, you can buy conical hats here and traditional wooden clogs made in the Hang Hom village.

In 1928-29 the Youth Revolution Comrade Association met in a tobacco shop at Number 15.

Turn left into Hang Thiec Street.

HÀNG THIẾC

TIN STREET

Hang Thiec was originally a village called Yen Noi. Before the French colonial period, the village produced religious items in cast pewter; lamps, candle holders, incense burners, kettles, cups and engraved pewter trays. Antique pewter can be found here. Metal products in brass, copper, iron and stainless steel are crafted on the pavement. The southern end of the street sells hammers, bolt cutters, screwdrivers, screws, nails, bolts, blades and scissors. Most houses here are built in the ancient matchbox style; beams made from ironwood and small mezzanine galleries. The lower floors are prone to flooding during monsoon season.

Hang Thiec Street turns into Thuoc Bac Street.

THUỐC BẮC

CHINESE HERB STREET

For a decade, traditional Chinese and Vietnamese medicinal herbs were sold here. Later, the herb shops moved to Lang Ong. The street was originally called Hang Lock Street. During the French colonial period, the market sold iron products; iron pipes, iron sheets and locks. As you walk north today, artisans solder, hammer and beat metal pieces right on the pavement. Retail shops here sell imported metal hardware goods; tools, safes, pots and locks.

Turn left into Hang Vai.

HÀNG VẢI

This street sold brown fabric for tunics. The French colonial and art deco houses, with antique facades, ornate plastered balconies and wooden shutters, have been restored. This street is famous for bamboo products. The signs with the names of the original owners have faded, but giant bamboo poles line both sides of the street.

Number 43 is the communal house dedicated to the god Tran. Number 44 is the communal house dedicated to the White Horse. Number 45 was the publishing house for the daily newspaper Garde.

Turn right into Hang Dong Street.

HÀNG ĐỒNG

COPPER STREET

In Hang Dong Street, traditional craftsmen made copper platters, casseroles, pots and pans for the royal courts. Later artisans improved their skills and made complex products such as antique trays, bird statues, incense burners, candle holders and singing bowls.

Today workshops make similar traditional objects and iron balustrades, handrails, copper sign boards and doors. A number of shops sell the famous Phuc Loc Tho porcelain.

Go straight on as Hang Dong runs into Bat Su. Turn left into Hang Ma Street.

HÀNG MÃ

Also known as Lantern Street; selling traditional Hoi Anh style lanterns, wood and paper lamps, outdoor lanterns and the silk lotus shaped lamps that are synonymous with Vietnam. Locals buy incense, religious votives and traditional funeral maps for their ancestors here.

Marriage invitations, business cards and flyers are designed and printed in shops all along this street. Quality standards are high. Check their samples.

Sheets of paper; plain, colored, art paper, striped, dotted, imported or handmade can also be purchased on Hang Ma.

Turn left into Phung Hung Street.

PHÙNG HƯNG

Phung Hung is named after a general who stormed the ancient citadel and became the king in the 8th century. He was known as the great father king who returned the country to prosperity and peace.

This street used to run the length of the eastern wall of the ancient citadel. The walls of the citadel were destroyed by the French in 1897, to make way for the railway. The railway you see today, is built on the foundation walls of the ancient citadel. The houses in the street are only odd numbers, because the even numbered houses were demolished and replaced by railway tracks.

At night, this is a popular street for locals to dine out on Lau dishes. Lau restaurants feature communal cooking. Broth is heated over a gas burner in the middle of the table. Food such as fish, crab, frog, beef, pork and vegetables are dropped into the simmering pot and cooked by guests around the table. Often, commuter trains flash by along the railway tracks, just meters away from the restaurants.

Turn left into Hang Vai.

HÀNG VẢI

FABRIC STREET

You are now back into Hang Vai Street, but at the other end of the street. This is typically the Old Quarter layout, where roads and alleys connect, intersect and cross back over each other. In the past, this street sold brown fabric for tunics. Now, the well-preserved antique houses; facades, cornices, tiles, doors, shutters and balconies, draw attention from locals, tourists, historians and photographers alike. This street is famous for bamboo products. The signs with the names of the original owners have faded, but giant bamboo poles for sale, line both sides of the street.

Number 7 is the entrance to a communal house. Number 43 is the communal house dedicated to the god Tran. Number 44 is the communal house dedicated to the White Horse. Number 45 was the publishing house for the daily newspaper Garde.

Turn right into Hang Ga.

HANG GÀ

CHICKEN STREET

Hang Ga Street is named after the bird trade, (Ga meaning chicken/bird). If you had walked here forty years ago, you would have seen houses selling ducks, geese, chickens, turkeys and birds. This area also sold herbs and opiate drugs.

Today there are printing shops specializing in wedding invitations and business cards. Number 16D is a communal house. Go through a corner door which has been cut into the white plaster wall and you'll enter a small courtyard with banyan trees. Here there is a small temple dedicated to the White Horse God of Hanoi.

Walk down Hang Ga Street into Hang Dieu Street.

HÀNG ĐIẾU

TOBACCO AND PIPE STREET

This street was once known as The Fire Place, due to the number of fires recorded in this area. In the 18th century, the fire problem was so bad, the government banned fire lighting at night; including lamps, pipes, cigarettes and water-pipe smoking. The fire ban was a problem for shop keepers, as Hang Dieu was a street full of tobacco shops. In The Spirit Fire Temple at number 30, a warning bell was hung. When a fire was ablaze, the bell was rung, alerting the locals.

The oldest profession in the world, carried on in the evenings at Number 76 and 82. Later the street diversified into leather goods; saddles, shoes and leather furniture were produced in the houses. The backyards had lime pools for curing hides.

Today shops sell leather shoes, cotton blankets, mattresses, pillows, bedding, jasmine tea and lotus jam. Lotus seed jam is a speciality of Hanoi. Drinking jasmine tea, while enjoying a plate of lotus seed jam, is to experience the taste of the real Hanoi.

Hang Dieu has speciality eel restaurants, popular with the locals. The eels are small and come from the surrounding cane fields on the outskirts of Hanoi. Fresh herb salads are served with crunchy fried strips of eel and spicy chili dressing, or soup and vermicelli with crispy eel.

Number 66 and 77 have historic architectual merit, with ornate filigree colonial edifices of a time when Hanoi was described as the Paris of the east.

Go straight on into Hang Da Street.

HÀNG DA

LEATHER STREET

This was also known as Fortune Tellers Street. The fortune tellers would sit outside Tan Thanh temple at number 40 and offer to tell the worshipers their fortunes for money. Now the locals call number 40 the voodoo house.

During the Nguyen dynasty 1802-1945, Hang Da market sold fresh produce and live cattle. The locals processed raw buffalo and ox hides, then tanned the hides and made artesian bags.

Local craftsmen today make and sell leather goods from buffalo, crocodile, ostrich and snake skin. In Hang Da you can buy designer bags, shoes, belts and briefcases. With no duty here, these high fashion leather goods can be a real bargain.

Turn left into Hang Bong Street.

HÀNG BÔNG

COTTON STREET

I n the 17th-18th century, Tay Son Trinh Lords bought gifts for the king in Hang Bong Street. Hang Bong Street is unusual because it crosses a few ancient villages. When you walk down Hang Bong Street, the lanes to the left or right take you into the original village streets.

The villages of Hang Bong traded in fine cotton, blankets, cushions and pillows. Workshops for cotton production have turned into retail shops selling fashion clothing, embroidered sheets, smocked dresses, finely embroidered table napkins, tablecloths and quilts made by women in the embroidery villages.

Bolts of cotton cloth are imported from China, Italy and Ireland, then hand embroidered in Vietnam. To determine quality, ask the shop-keeper about the origins of the fabric.

Turn right into Ly Quoc Su Street.

LÝ QUỐC SƯ

Ly Quoc Su Street is the old village of Tien Thi. The French called it Rue Lamblot.

There are two pagoda's in this street. The most famous one is the ancient Ba Da Pagoda (Stone Lady). At the time of Le Thanh Tong's reign (1460 – 1497), a stone deity was discovered in the shape of a female goddess. A small shrine was built where the statue was found. The villagers became frightened of the deity, so they made the shrine into a pagoda and invited monks to look after it.

The pagoda has been rebuilt many times. Two solid cast bells, (circa1823 and 1881) plus a gong made in 1842 can be seen there.

A small family run samosa restaurant is right next door to the pagoda. This is one of the most famous street food places in Hanoi.

You will find music and mobile phone stores here and some of the best souvenir and international designer fashion shops in Hanoi.

Another local institution and hangout is Joma café which supports socially disadvantaged young people in the community. Through the courtyard, there is an air-conditioned space with leather sofas for lounging, magazines and filtered water in jugs. Clean bathrooms too.Joma serves up great freshly ground coffee and real pumpkin pie.

If you want a break from Vietnamese food, take note of the locations of the five star European restaurants in this street. These restaurants carry a world-class range of wines and beers.

We finish this walk in the Cathedral Square.

CATHEDRAL WALK

DISTANCE: 2.5 KILOMETERS. TIME: APPROX 2-3 HOUR WALK.

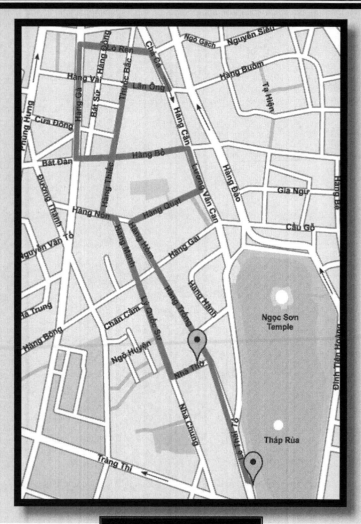

NHÀ THỜ

CATHEDRAL STREET

Nha Tho is a traditional Old Quarter Street in the center of the city. This open, sunlight, leafy-green urban space is filled with character and charm. This is the French catholic district with St Joseph's Cathedral, a magnificent Roman Catholic Church, at its centre. Two bell towers wake the locals in the mornings and ring the hours of each passing day. Buttresses, doorways, stained glass windows and domes are designed around the gothic style architecture of historic Paris cathedrals. After the cathedral first opened its doors in 1886, Cathedral Street has always been crowded with hundreds of people. Local people and tourists hang out with friends; drinking, talking, attending church, taking wedding photos, and of course...people watching.

This street is now known as lemon tea street, as it's a popular place in the evening for young people to sit and drink tea with friends.

We suggest you start this walking tour at Moca Café in Nha Tho Street. From the French mosaic tiled floors, Parisian style cafe chairs, to the carved dark wood bar, exposed bricks, classic photos and ceiling fans, the cafe retains the atmosphere of French colonial days. A great place for people watching with a cup of fresh brewed Robusta coffee.

This street is fifty meters long, with some of the best restaurants packed into this strip; French, Italian and an American style rib joint. The French Bakery serves authentic French patisseries and an Italian guy runs the Italian restaurant, which does great authentic wood-fired pizzas and hand-made pastas.

Shop in Nha Tho for Vietnamese souvenirs and gifts of quality at reasonable prices. A good place to buy gifts that people actually like. Award-winning designers produce well-cut, unfussy clothing for the boutiques around here. Ipa-Nima sells kitschy, girly bags and whimsical accessories; La Casa sells traditional crafts; Mosaique is a little boutique designer shop selling silver jewelry, silk hangings, clothing and home furnishings; Ngu sells exquisite linens, silks and clothing to fulfill your wish list; Things of Substance has original designs in western dress sizes in cotton and linen with a touch of eastern influence; Three Trees is a jewelry design store owned by a Belgium expat.

Turn right into Ly Quoc Su Street.

LÝ QUỐC SƯ

L y Quoc Su Street is the old village of Tien Thi. The French called it Rue Lamblot.

There are two pagoda's in this street. The most famous one is the ancient Ba Da Pagoda (Stone Lady). At the time of Le Thanh Tong's reign (1460 – 1497), a stone deity was discovered in the shape of a female goddess. A small shrine was built where the statue was found. However the villagers became frightened of the deity and to satisfy the spirits they made the shrine into a pagoda and invited monks to look after it.

The pagoda has been rebuilt many times. Two solid cast bells, (circa1823 and 1881) plus a gong made in 1842 can be seen there.

A small family run samosa restaurant is right next door to the pagoda. This is one of the most famous street food places in Hanoi.

You will find music and mobile phone stores here and some of the best souvenir and international designer fashion shops in Hanoi.

Another local institution and hangout is Joma café which supports socially disadvantaged young people in the community. Through the courtyard, there is an air-conditioned space with leather sofas for lounging, magazines and filtered water in jugs. Clean bathrooms too.Joma serves up great freshly ground coffee and real pumpkin pie.

If you want a break from Vietnamese food, take note of the locations of the five star European restaurants in this street. These restaurants carry a world-class range of wines and beers.

Carry straight on as this street runs into Hang Manh Street.

HÀNG MÀNH

BAMBOO BLIND STREET

O ver a hundred years ago, craftsmen from the Te Yen Phong district, brought bamboo blind making and cork floor manufacturing to Hang Manh Street. Today, four families still follow the ancestral craft, making blinds for doors and windows.

Hang Manh Street in the 1920's and 1930's was home to several infamous licensed brothels. In 1938, at the height of the resistance against the French colonists, the house at Number 1 was the secret base of the resistance group called Hoang Van Thu.

After 1920, real estate values in Hang Manh rose. Local owners and developers started renovating and preserving the old houses.

Turn left into Hang Non Street.

HÀNG NÓN

CONICAL HAT STREET

Traditional conical hats for men were made from pineapple leaves or feathers with a silver or copper knob at the top. Noble women wore wide flat palm leaf hats with fringes called Nghe. On labor sites today, workers wear conical hats, known as the Non La (leaf hat). The hat has become an iconic symbol. They are extremely versatile. Primarily used as protection from the sun and rain. When dipped in water, it becomes an evaporative cooling device. It is used as a basin to carry water or rice; a fan for a ploughman on a hot summer's day; a basket to carry a bunch of vegetables from the market and for romantic couples to hide behind to steal a kiss. Today, you can still buy conical hats here and traditional wooden clogs made in Hang Hom village.

In 1928-29 the Youth Revolution Comrade Association met in a tobacco shop at Number 15.

Turn right into Hang Thiec Street.

HÀNG THIẾC

TIN STREET

Hang Thiec was originally a village called Yen Noi. Before the French colonial period, the village produced religious items in cast pewter; lamps, candle holders, incense burners, kettles, cups and engraved pewter trays.

Today metal products in brass, copper, iron and stainless steel are crafted on the pavement. The southern end of the street sells hammers, bolt cutters, screwdrivers, screws, nails, bolts, blades and scissors.

Most houses here are built in the ancient matchbox style; beams made from ironwood and small mezzanine galleries. The lower floors are prone to flooding, during monsoon season.

Carry straight on into Thuoc Bac Street.

THUỐC BẮC

I n the early 20th century traditional Chinese and Vietnamese medicinal herbs were sold here. Now the herb shops have moved around the corner to Lan Ong Street.

During the French colonial era the street was called Hang Lock Street. Metal objects are sold here today. As you walk north, shops sell hand crafted metal barbecues, cabinetry, tools, safes, pots, locks and mirrors. Some designs, like scroll legged cafe chairs and tables, echo the French colonial past.

Turn right into Lan Ong Street.

LÃN ÔNG

TRADITIONAL MEDICINE STREET

L an Ong is named after a learned mandarin scholar who wrote sixty-three traditional oriental medicine books.

Pungent earthy aromas fill the street. The shops sell herbs, teas, roots and dried fruits. Here illnesses and ailments are diagnosed by natural medicine doctors trained in traditional medicine diagnosis and healing methods. Prescribed herbs are selected from small wooden drawers or glass jars, weighed and measured; then wrapped in paper packages and tied with twine. Verbal instructions are given on how to prepare a tea or infusion with the herbs, bark, seeds and fungi.

Aside from medicinal healing, there are special herb teas with specific properties to promote health, longevity, increase stamina, prevent flu's and colds and promote beauty. Tea is an important ceremony and part of the Vietnamese culture. From the bitter artichoke root tea, to the fragrant lotus and chrysan-themum teas blooming in china cups, as steaming hot water is poured.

Today there are fifty-one traditional medicine outlets. Many of the shops have had the tradition of selling oriental medicinal herbs passed down through the generations. Shops around here also sell vita-mins and quality skin care products: pharmaceutical drugs for migraine, heart medication, ointments, ste-roid creams, anti-depressants and Viagra are sold on request, without prescription. For tourists in the medi-cal profession, it's a jaw-dropping experience seeing what is sold on the streets.

Turn left into Cha Ca Street.

CHẢ CÁ

✂ *GRILLED FISH STREET*

I n 1885 the Doan family, opened a restaurant at number 14 Hang Son Street called 'Cha Ca La Vong'. The restaurant featured a signature dish of butter-coated barbecued fish, cooked at the table, with dill, turmeric and spring onions with peanuts, vermicelli noodles, a secret sauce and herb salad on the side. The dish was so well appreciated by the local Hanoi people, they named the street after the fish dish. The restaurant at number 14 has been serving their famous grilled fish dishes for over one hundred years. Note the old wooden staircase and family antiques. In the restaurant, there's a statue of La Vong, an old fisherman, with a rod in one hand and a fishing line dangling in the other.

Turn left into Lo Ren Street.

LÒ RÈN

L o Ren Street was home to blacksmiths forging metal tools and household objects for the royal citadel. They also made hoes and harrows, so the street became known as 'Hoe and Harrow Street'. Number 1 is the communal house that worships the ancestor of metallurgy.

During the French colonial occupation, the French built houses, commercial buildings, government buildings, railways, tramways, stores and bridges. The nuts, bolts and iron doors for French colonial developers, were forged in Lo Ren Street. You can still see traditional blacksmith products at number 26.

Walk to the end of Lo Ren, turn left into Hang Ga.

HÀNG GA

CHICKEN STREET

Hang Ga is named after the bird trade, (Ga meaning chicken/bird). If you had walked down Hang Ga Street forty years ago, you would see houses selling ducks, geese, chickens, turkeys and birds in bamboo cages. Herbs and opiate drugs were also sold here, until the 1920's. Today there are printing shops specializing in wedding invitations and business cards.

Turn left into Bat Dan Street.

BÁT ĐÀN

PORCELAIN BOWL STREET

In the early 20th century, even numbered houses sold clay bowls that were brought to the city from riverside workshops on the Red River. Odd numbers sold leather and wood items. Number 33 is an ornate communal house of architectural merit. For culinary interest, stop in at number 49 Bat Dan Street for a bowl of the famous Hanoi pho (soup). This restaurant uses a much prized secret family recipe.

Carry straight on into Hang Bo Street.

HÀNG BỒ

BAMBOO BASKET STREET

Hang Bo has small traditional houses where bamboo baskets, clogs and sandals were sold. Now Hang Bo sells needles, thread, beads, buttons, zippers and clippers. There is a French bakery and cake shop at number 20.

In the evening, all vendor stalls disappear and mats are thrown on the footpaths, where locals meet with friends to eat barbecued cuttlefish, dried squid and drink cold beer.

Turn right into Luong Van Can Street.

LƯƠNG VĂN CAN

The street is named after Luong Van Can (1854-1927). He was a Vietnamese mandarin, school administrator, independence activist and writer. A propagandist and patriotic agitator against the French colonial rule. His most noted work is Nha nuoc, *The State*. In 1907, he co-founded the famous Dong Kinh Nghia Thuc (Tonkin Free School). The school printed books calling for innovative policies and new ways of thinking to enhance the education and intelligence of the people. He was arrested by the French and exiled to Con Dao Island. He died on June 12, 1927 at number 4 Hang Dao Street. The houses from number 6 - 18 were used as the first Tuong Opera Theatre in Hanoi. Now known as The Thang Long Music and Dance Theatre.

Near the end of the street childrens' games, toys and stuffed animals are sold. You can buy the traditional women's dress called Ao Dai at Number 6 and number 8. These long dresses, with petite mandarin collars, two slits up the side are usually worn over flowing silk pants.

The shop owners in this street migrated from the village called Truch Xa. Consequently most of the shop names include the word Truch, for example, An Truch, Phuc Truch, Binh Truch, Hung Truch. This is the way local people still keep close ties to their villages.

Turn right into Hang Quat Street.

HÀNG QUẠT

FAN STREET

Hang Quat Street sold paper fans made by the villagers in Dao Xa (Top Fan). In the French colonial period, it was called 'rue des Eventails' (Hang Fans). Today Hang Quat sells ceremonial decorations for ancestral shrines, prayer flags and wood blocks for printing prayer papers. This is an important street for local people as the daily ceremony of ancestor worship is performed in every home and shop. Shrines are adorned with worldly offerings for the family ancestors.

Number 4 is a communal house honoring the founder of fan making. It is also a memorial to the martyrs who died in the French colonial period. Number 43 was the first private school for continuing education. Number 64 is a popular temple for worship; The Dau temple, dedicated to Mother Saint of Hanoi, Lieu Hanh.

Turn left into Hang Hom.

HÀNG HÒM

In the 19th century, wood craftsmen produced black stained wooden trunks for clothing and multi-drawer chests for paper storage. They engraved wooden alter panels and made small box-es for holding betel leaves and areca nuts. Later, the woodwork was decorated with lacquer, using the res-in of the special tree, rhus succedanea.

In the 1930's, Vietnamese artists, in collaboration with French artists, developed a distinct genre of fine art painting, sometimes applying more than ten lay-ers or more of black, red, brown or clear lacquer.

Today the tradition of lacquer art is still a com-mercial and cultural activity in Hang Hom. The Com-munal House at number 11, was constructed for wor-shiping Tra Lu, the ancestor of lacquer painting.

Go straight on into Hang Trong Street.

HÀNG TRỐNG

This street was part of the dike for the Red river. Many small villages set up here to make drums, parasols, awnings and canopies. Hang Trong was also famous for folk wood art and block prints.

The shops in Hang Trong sell arts and crafts and fine silk products. Many art galleries here today exhibit work by local artists. You will also see artists at work in the shops, copying works of the great masters and Impressionists. There is a heady smell of oil paint coming from shop doorways, as local artists are busy working on canvases.

There are two ancient temples here. The first one at number 82 is dedicated to a talented singer. She had a successful singing career and used her earnings to support the poor. The narrow temple at number 82 is built directly over her tomb. The second temple (upstairs at number 75) is Huong temple. Dedicated to the four directional gods of Hanoi city: Tran

Vu, Bach Ma, Linh Lang and Cao Son.

Carry on down Hang Trong Street until you see Hoan Kiem Lake on your left. The street that runs along the side of the lake here is called Le Thai To Street. One side of the road is a lake side walk and the other is a shopping walk.

On the right hand side of the road, stores sell more genuine international brands in one hundred meters, than anywhere else in Hanoi. From Gucci to Chanel and Cartier; from Fendi to Hermes, it's an international designer shopping mecca.

Number 48 Fanny's ice-cream, is a famous French ice-cream parlor. Across the road, is Hoan Kiem Lake. The cafe beside the lake is a relaxing place to unwind at the end of this walk.

THE FRENCH QUARTER WALK

DISTANCE: 3 KILOMETERS. TIME: APPROX 2-4 HOUR WALK.

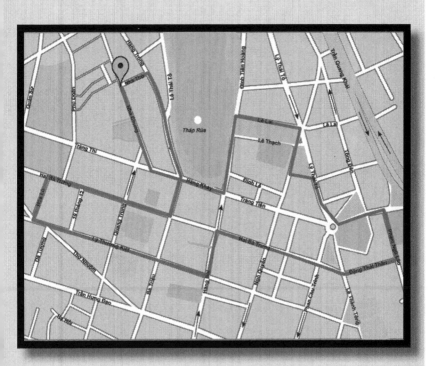

After the busy narrow streets of the Old Quarter, the French Quarter has wide tree lined boulevards and pavements. The French Quarter has architecture from different eras; ancient pagodas, international modern, classical European, avant-garde art deco residences and oriental French architecture from colonial times. The buildings reflect the influences of the French, Vietnamese and Soviet cultures of the day.

NHÀ THỜ

CATHEDRAL STREET

The walk starts in Nha Tho Street. It is a traditional Old Quarter Street in the center of the city. This open, sunlight, leafy-green urban space is filled with character and charm. This is the French catholic district, with St Joseph's Cathedral, a magnificent Roman Catholic Church at its centre. Two bell towers wake the locals in the mornings and ring the hours of each passing day. Buttresses, doorways, stained glass windows and domes are designed around the gothic style architecture of historic Paris cathedrals. After the cathedral first opened its doors in 1886, Cathedral Street has always been crowded with hundreds of people. Local people and tourists hang out with friends; drinking, talking, attending church, taking wedding photos, and of course... people watching.

This street is now known as lemon tea street, a popular place in the evenings for young people to sit and drink tea with friends.

We suggest you start this walking tour at Moca Café. From the French mosaic tiled floors, Parisian style cafe chairs, to the carved dark wood bar, exposed bricks, classic photos and ceiling fans, the cafe retains the atmosphere of French colonial days. A great place for people watching with a cup of fresh brewed Robusta coffee.

This street is fifty meters long, with some of the best restaurants packed into this strip; French, Italian and an American style rib joint. The French Bakery serves authentic French patisseries and an Italian guy runs the Italian restaurant, which does great authentic wood-fired pizzas and hand-made pastas.

Shop in Nha Tho for Vietnamese souvenirs and gifts of quality at reasonable prices. A good place to buy gifts that people actually like. Award-winning designers produce well-cut, unfussy clothing for the boutiques around here. Ipa-Nima sells kitschy, girly bags and whimsical accessories; La Casa sells traditional crafts; Mosaique is a little boutique designer shop selling silver jewelry, silk hangings, clothing and home furnishings; Ngu sells exquisite linens, silks and clothing to fulfill your wish list; Things of Substance has original designs in western dress sizes in cotton and linen with a touch of eastern influence. At the end of the street turn left into Nha Chung Street.

NHÀ CHUNG

TOGETHER HOUSE

The name of this street came into history when the French turned the Bao Thien Tu village land, (where the cathedral and Nga Chung Street are located) into the common property of the Catholic church. The Vietnamese and French called the street associated to this area Nga Chung, *Together House*.

The area was used as a centre for the administration and management of church property; houses, printing shops and craft workshops.

Saint Joseph Cathedral was built on the foundation of the Bao Thien Pagoda and was completed around 1886. With its neo-gothic architecture, Saint Joseph has been a place of contemplation for more than one hundred years. Sitting inside for a concert or church service, is like being transported back to 1886 France.

A pedestrian paradise, the tree lined square

forms a central plaza known for its open air cafes. The place to soak up the Old Quarter's oriental atmosphere. Walking down the street you'll come across souveniers, propaganda posters, fashion, toys, stationery, fast food, silk, lacquer and the Peoples Park.

At the end of Nha Chung Street turn left into Trang Thi Street.

TRANG THI

This part of Tran Thi street has a couple of excellent antique shops selling old gothic French and Vietnamese antiques. The cane furniture and tribal woven basket shops.

Opposite the cane shops, on the corner of Trang Thi and Le Thai To, is a French colonial administration building of architectural interest.

Go straight on into Hang Khay Street.

HÀNG KHAY

Famous for selling chairs, wardrobes, tables and couches in the 13th century. In the 18th century the French named it rue des Incrusteurs (street of engravers). After 1954, it was renamed and is now called Hang Khay. Today it caters for tourists wanting watches, jewelry and electronics.

Then turn left at the end of Hoan Kiem lake into Dinh Tien Hoang Street.

ĐINH TIÊN HOÀNG

Dinh Tien Hoang was named after the emperor who vanquished twelve warlords. This heralded the Dinh Dynasty, which brought peace to the country in 968.

The lake you are walking around is one of the

central points of Hanoi. Every morning, from 5.30am till 7am, Thai Chi and traditional fan dances are performed by the locals. This practice goes back to the time of the Le Dynasty, six centuries ago, when the legend of the lake was created.

Ask any local about the legend of the lake and the story they tell you, goes like this. During the war against the Chinese Minh Dynasty, the Vietnamese king, Le Thai To was given a magical sword by the Golden Turtle God from the lake in the middle of Hanoi, known as Luc Thuy (meaning green water). After ten years of war, the King finally defeated the Chinese and reclaimed the nations independence.

Some time later, while the King Le Thai To was boating on Luc Thuy Lake, a large turtle swam towards him, took the sword, submerged and disappeared. The king realized that the Golden Turtle God of the lake must have presented the sword for the sole purpose of defeating the Chinese. In reverence, he named the Lake Ho Hoan Kiem or Lake of the Restored Sword. The Turtle Tower *Thap Rua* standing on a small island near the centre of the lake, is linked closely to the legend.

Towards the northern end of the lake, there's the

ancient and mythical temple, Den Ngoc Son, Temple of the Jade Mountain. This temple honors the 13th century military leader Tran Hung Dao, who defeated the Mongols of the Yuan Dynasty. The island, on which the temple sits, is called Jade Island. To access the temple, you cross the red wooden Huc Bridge (Huc translates to morning sunlight). Picture postcard perfect; the red bridge, the jade water below, morning mist and peach blossoms.

Along Dinh Tien Hoang, there is a memorial park called Ly Thai To Park. The golden statue of Ly Thai To, towers over the park and marble tiled square. Loudspeakers blast out dance music, early morning and in the evening for mass aerobic sessions. This is a chance to get together with a hundred Vietnamese doing aerobics in the park.

Beside the park is Le Lai Street. Turn right into Le Lai Street, then right into Ngo Quyen.

NGÔ QUYẼN

N go Quyen Street is named after a general who later became the King of Vietnam. He defeated Southern Han invaders in the Bach Dang River, ending one thousand years of occupation by the Chinese.

The engineer Gustave Eiffel, who designed the Eiffel Tower in Paris, also designed much of the ornate metal French structures (balconies, entrances, porticoes) you see in Ngo Quyen. Ornate fences and gates can be seen in the building opposite the Metropole Hotel.

Look for Le Phung Hien Street next to the Metropole Hotel. Turn left into Le Phung Hien.

LÊ PHUNG HIỂU

The landmark is The Hotel Metropole. A French style colonial hotel with classical white facade, green shutters and original wrought iron detail. This hotel is one of the few remaining hotels of its era in Vietnam.

Built in 1901 by two private French investors, the hotel quickly became the rendez-vous point for colonial society, in the first half of the century. Following Vietnamese independence in the 1950's, the new national government opted to maintain it as the official hotel for visiting VIPs. During and after the war years it became a base for press and diplomats.

The hotel guest list has included Presidents, Dukes, Prime Ministers, as well as the rich and famous: Catherine Deneuve, Charlie Chaplin, Jane Fonda, Stephen Hawking, Oliver Stone, Mick Jagger, Sir Roger Moore amongst others.

Graham Green wrote 'The Quiet American' here. Somerset Maugham wrote 'The Gentleman in the Parlour' at the hotel.

The hotel welcomes visitors anytime. You don't have to be a hotel guest to enjoy a drink at the pool bar or the Hemingway bar or join in a cooking class in the kitchen.

Turn right into Ly Thai To Street.

LÝ THÁI TỔ

The buildings in this street reflect the French colonial era and expatriate life in Hanoi. On the left you'll see The Press Club, once the famed hangout of journalists and expats. On the menu is the original style American burger and traditional English pub beef pie.

Walk until you reach the busy round about. Look across the road and you'll see the Hanoi Opera House. Built by two French architects Harlay and Broyer in 1901, completed in 1911. Modeled on the Palais Garnier (the famous Paris opera house) this gracious building is considered to be one of the architectural landmarks of Hanoi.

Trang Tien Street runs down the left hand side of the Opera House.

TRÀNG TIỀN

At the end of Trang Tien Street, The National Historical Museum is one of the most impressive oriental French colonial style buildings of its style. When it opened in 1932, it was called the Louis Finot Museum. The museum exhibited extensive collections of ancient artifacts sourced from Southeast Asia. In 1958, four years after the French loss of Indochina, France gave the building to Vietnam, and it became the National Historical Museum. The museum exhibits thousands of artifacts, displayed in order of antiquity, from ancient to contemporary. Well worth an hour to look around.

Turn right into Pham Ngu Lao.

PHAM NGU LÀO

Pham Ngu Lao is dominated by the Military Academy where major military receptions are held. The architecture is French colonial style. This entire area is owned by the military, including the hotels and swimming pools. While the tall gates and guardhouse look imposing, don't let this put you off. Visitors are welcome to look through the military museum and swim in the pools. Both are open to the public. The pools are a quiet retreat on a hot Hanoi day and are popular with tourists, locals and expatriates. You can buy a pool pass and hire towels at the hotel reception desk. Sit poolside on loungers under shady songbird trees.

Turn right into Dang Thai Than Street.

DANG THAI THAN

The Hanoi Hilton Hotel towers above this street. In the lobby, you can buy a ticket for the fitness centre and roof-top swimming pool. Order lunch or drinks by the pool, or in the restaurant and cafes inside the main foyer.

Across the road, there are factory outlet shops that sell clothing. Brand clothes are produced in Vietnam and exported to Europe and the U.S.A. With over-runs, end of season, samples and slightly imperfect garments, one can find top brands here at bargain prices.

Walk straight ahead then over the cross road into Hai Ba Trung Street.

HAI BÀ TRUNG

All along Hai Ba Trung, you'll find electronic stores and interesting French oriental architecture. At number 22 Hai Ba Trung, there is a unique boutique cinema, called Cinematheque Theatre. To get there, walk up the alley at Number 22, past the guard minding the parked motorbikes (25 meters), turn right and you'll come to the theatre and bar. If you have time, catch one of the sessions of foreign films, alternative films and Vietnamese documentaries. This theatre, run by an expat, has survived its share of censorship closures. Still the projectors are running.

The enclave is typical of the French colonial style with budget hotel rooms upstairs. In the evening snacks, beer, wine, coffee and the anise-flavored spirit absinthe are sold across the ornate wood bar in the courtyard. All of which you can take into the cinema. Lanterns above festoon the canopy of the ancient blossom tree. The place is little run down now, but full of atmosphere, especially in the evening when the expats get together at one of their favorite places in town. Turn left into Hang Bai Street.

HÀNG BÀI

Hang Bai is a street full of audio and electronic equipment. The first lane on your left has professional camera equipment for sale.

Turn right into Ly Thuong Kiet Street.

LÝ THƯƠNG KIỆT

This street is named after a famous general. The Vietnamese Women's Museum at number 36 is well worth a visit. It's a unique lens into the Vietnamese women's way of life. Photographic displays and exhibitions highlight traditional dress through the centuries; give insights into village life; marriage, birth, food, games, death and traditional ceremonies. On one floor, discover the role of women patriot spies and fighting women during the French colonial times and the American war. An overall historical and social focus of Vietnamese women: their medicines, folklore, handicrafts, jewelry, photos, letters and books are on display.

On the corner of Ly Thuong Kiet and Hoa Lo Street, The High Court stands opposite the Hoa Lo Prison, (the infamous Hanoi Hilton). The court building is a magnificent, example of oriental French colonial style architecture. The Vietnamese government has kept the building in its original form. Note the use of traditional lime wash pigment paint on the walls.

In this part of the city, many colonial administration buildings have been restored to their original glory. Walk up Da Tuong Street (opposite the gates of the High Court) and you will be near the alley where we lived. At the end of this detour, you'll come to Tran Hung Dao where there are various buildings of the Oriental colonial style; wrought iron balconies, painted French shutters and imposing filigree iron gates.

Back on Ly Thuong Kiet by the High Court, turn right into Hoa Lo Street.

HOẢ LÒ

HELL HOLE

The name Hoa Lo, commonly translated as 'hell hole', or 'stove'. The name originated from the concentration of stores selling wood stoves and coal-fire stoves in pre-colonial times.

On the left hand side, stands Hoa Lo Prison. The prison was used by the French colonists to lock up political prisoners. Street peddlers made money by passing messages in through the jail's windows and tossing tobacco and opium over the walls. Letters and packets would be thrown out in the opposite direction. During the 1930's and 1940's, many of the future leading figures in Communist North Vietnam spent time in Maison Centrale, as it was called by the French. North Vietnam incarcerated allied prisoners here during the Vietnam War. Sarcastically known to American prisoners of war as the 'Hanoi Hilton'. The prison was demolished in the 1990's and a shopping center, apartments and hotel were built on the site.

Only the gatehouse inside the original wall remains today and is now kept as a museum. There are a range of prison artifacts on display, the most famous collections are photographs and memorabilia from the American war.

Turn right into Hai Ba Trung Street.

HAI BÀ TRƯNG

Hai Ba Trung is a commercial street selling the latest home appliances; juicers, slow cookers, 82 inch flat screen digital televisions, refrigerators, the latest electronic phones and must-have gadgets. Turn left into Ba Trieu Street.

BÀ TRIỆU

O nce you reach Ba Trieu Street, you are on you way back. Keep on the left side of the road. At the end of Ba Trieu, you'll be at the southern end of Hoan Kiem Lake in Le Thai To Street. This street runs parallel to the lake, which will be on your right.

Go straight on into Le Thai To.

LÊ THÁI TỔ

A long the left hand side of the road, you'll find the most dreamy of luxury stores selling more international brands in this one hundred meter shopping strip, than anywhere else in Hanoi. With shops like Chanel, you can browse and buy haute couture. Turn left into Nha Tho Street and you are back where you began.

THE MYSTICAL LAKE WALK

DISTANCE: 3 KILOMETERS. TIME: APPROX 2-3 HOUR WALK.

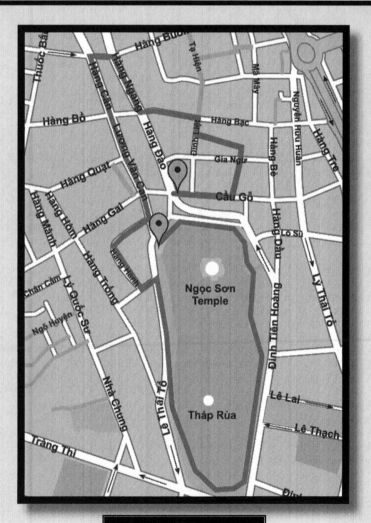

CẦU GÔ

WOOD BRIDGE STREET

The name reflects the original function of the street. A bridge over the waters. French colonists reclaimed Hang Dao Lake, Taiji Lake and Hoan Kiem Lake tributaries, for land development. The bridge, creek and two lakes all disappeared. Now, the only remaining lake is Hoan Kiem.

The first pho restaurant opened in Hanoi on Cau Go Street. Pho is a famous street food in Vietnam; a noodle soup consisting of broth, rice noodles, fresh herbs, and beef or chicken. Now so famous, this dish is served in speciality restaurants from Sydney to Paris.

Cau Go Street is still a popular food mecca. If you want to eat like a true local, this is the place. You can pull up a chair and eat pho; rice or vermicelli with chicken; steamed sticky rice cakes with special herbs, rice cakes filled with meat, onions and mushrooms. At night, street food stalls and small restaurants offer barbecued seafood, from the port of Hai Phong.

Look out for a market lane called Ngo Cau Go off the main street. This is an authentic lane, typical of local Hanoi life. In the early morning, Ngo Cau Go turns into a flower and fresh produce market. In the afternoon, vendors sell fresh beef, pork, chicken and often catfish, frogs, paddy-field crabs and freshwater snails. Home refrigeration has become more common, but the locals still like to ensure freshness by buying fresh produce every day (if not twice a day) to take home for lunch or evening meals.

At number 43 Cao Co, for the past fifty years, a family has been making a famous Hanoi dish called Bun Cha. A lunchtime dish served between 11am and 2pm. Small barbecued pork patties served on rice noodles in a bowl of fragrant broth, accompanied by side dishes of herb salad, fried spring rolls, garlic and chili pickles. The spring rolls (called cha gio), are made of seasoned ground meat, mushrooms, and diced carrots, kohlrabi and jicama, rolled up in rice paper, then deep fried until crispy. You have to ask the vendor for *cha gio*. Point to them,hold up your fingers to say how many.

This style of eating is so local, you can find yourself dining in someone's living room; television tuned into the Vietnamese news; the family alter, roses, oranges and incense burning. Make yourself at home (but don't stare or take photos of the alter).

Turn left into Cho Cau Go.

CHỢ CẦU GÔ

Cho Cau Go is a market street where the women sit in the alley selling vegetables, fruit and meat from baskets. Markets are busy before 9am and in the late afternoon. When the basket ladies aren't there, you'll see locals sitting in the alley outside each other's houses, talking, smoking and drinking tea. This is local life in Hanoi.

Follow this lane through until you come out at Dinh Liet Street.

ĐINH LIỆT

KNITTING STREET

Historically this has been the one stop street for haberdashery. There are still shops selling wool, needles, knitted sweaters and scarves. Dinh Liet also has boutique shops, specializing in beads, jewelry, silk scarves and bags.

7A Quan Bia Minh is a popular restaurant and cafe, with expats. Upstairs, in this French colonial house there is a shady veranda overlooking the street. Number 4B has a photo gallery with well-observed artistic photos of Vietnam.

Turn left into Hang Bac.

HÀNG BẠC

SILVER STREET

Hang Bac is one of the oldest streets in the Old Quarter, dating from the 13th century and has always honored the silversmith guild. During the French colonial period, Hang Bac Street was named Rue Des Changeurs, *city of money-changers.*

The street now has high-end jewelry shops selling both traditional and modern designer jewelry.

Number 42 is a communal house honoring the ancestors of silver smiths, dating back to the 16th century. Then number 58 was a forge for casting silver coins and bullion for the royal court. Today it is still a temple of worship, but it also holds traditional musical performances called Ca Tru. This style of musical performance dates back to the time of the ancient royal courts. If you wish to know more about Ca Tru refer to the web site at www.catru.com.vn.

Turn right into Hàng Ngang Street.

HÀNG NGANG

CROSS STREET

The Chinese Hau Le people formed Feudal courts in the late Le Dynasty which ruled the country from 1428 to 1788. At that time The Le emperors introduced and applied the Chinese system of civil service. Massive change then took place in Vietnamese society. The Buddhist state became Confucian, based on Chinese principles. The Chinese instigated all the civil laws. The Vietnamese Minh Huong people were the spiritual brokers who brought together Chinese religious worship and the traditional worship of the Vietnamese. This is illustrated at the Tam Thanh Temple, where both forms of belief are worshiped today.

Hang Ngang was an exclusive area and only the rich traded there. It still remains the busiest and most prosperous street in Hanoi. Number 7 and number 27 were homes of wealthy silk traders.

Number 48 is where Ho Chi Minh wrote the Vietnamese declaration of independence. This house is an historic revolutionary landmark.

Number 62 sells pearls from Phu Quoc Island (including highly sought after black pearls), and jade (known as the diamond of the North). They also have an extensive collection of traditional gold and silver jewelry, such as solid gold wedding necklaces. A Vietnamese bride is given a gold necklace on her wedding day. The idea being, if she finds herself on her own, she can sell the solid gold necklace.

Turn left into Lan Ong Street. We suggest you walk further up Lan Ong Street, about 50 meters, to see all the natural medicine stores. Then come back and go down Hang Can Street.

LÂN ÔNG

L an Ong is named after a learned mandarin scholar who wrote sixty-three traditional oriental medicine books.

Pungent earthy aromas fill the street. The shops sell herbs, teas, roots and dried fruits. Here illnesses and ailments are diagnosed by natural medicine doctors trained in traditional medicine diagnosis and healing methods. After the diagnosis, prescribed herbs are selected from small wooden drawers or glass jars, weighed and measured; then wrapped in paper packages and tied with twine. Verbal instructions are given on how to prepare a tea or infusion with the herbs, bark, seeds and fungi. Tea is an important ceremony and part of the Vietnamese culture. From the bitter artichoke root tea, to the fragrant lotus and chrysanthemum teas blooming in china cups, as water is poured. Aside from medicinal healing, there are special herb teas with specific properties to promote health, beauty, longevity, stamina, prevent flu's and colds.

Today there are fifty-one traditional medicine outlets. Many of the shops have had the tradition of selling oriental medicinal herbs passed down through the generations. Shops around here also sell vitamins and quality skin care products: pharmaceutical drugs for migraine, heart medication, ointments, steroid creams, anti-depressants and Viagra are sold on request, without prescription. For tourists in the medical profession, it's a jaw-dropping experience seeing what is sold on the streets.

Turn into Hang Can Street and carry on into Luong Van Can Street.

LƯƠNG VĂN CAN

The street is named after Luong Van Can (1854-1927). He was a Vietnamese mandarin, school administrator, independence activist, writer, propagandist and patriotic agitator against the French colonial rule. His most noted work is Nha nuoc, *The State*. In 1907, he co-founded the famous Dong Kinh Nghia Thuc (Tonkin Free School). The school printed books calling for innovative policies and new ways of thinking, to enhance the education and intelligence of the people. He was arrested by the French and exiled to Con Dao Island. He died on June 12, 1927 at number 4 Hang Dao Street.

The houses from number 6-18 were used as the first Tuong Opera Theatre in Hanoi. Now known as, The Thang Long Music and Dance Theatre. Near the end of the street, childrens' games, toys and stuffed animals are sold. The traditional women's dress called Ao Dai is sold at number 6 and number 8. These long dresses, with petite mandarin collars, two slits up the sides are usually worn over flowing silk pants.

The shop owners in this street migrated from the village called Truch Xa. Consequently most of the shop names include the word Truch, for example, An Truch, Phuc Truch, Binh Truch, Hung Truch. This is the way local people still keep close ties to their villages.

Go over Hang Gai Street and turn right into Hang Hanh Street.

HÀNG HÀNH

A nice walking lane, close to Hoan Kiem Lake. This characterful lane has bars, cafes, an authentic French bakery, pizzas, DVD shops, boutique hotels and travel agents. Number 11B The Apple Tart French bakery, make the best citron lemon tart we have tasted. Handmade chocolate covered candied orange rind, pear and almond tarts and French bread are also delicious. Silk shops in this street have some gorgeous hand embroidered clothes, silk scarves, cashmere shawls and soft furnishings. Turn left at Bao Khanh Street.

BÁO KHÁNH

During lunch time and evenings, there is a Banh Cuon street restaurant, that serves thin rice pancakes with a choice of fillings. The pancakes are cooked right infront of you and make a delicious snack. You'll find several western style restaurants in this area.

Turn right at Le Thai To Street.

LÊ THÁI TỔ

Directly opposite Bao Khanh is the lake side restaurant, Thuy Ta. Five hundred meters down the tree-lined street, on the right hand side of the road, boutique stores sell more international brands, than any where else in Hanoi. Designer brands from London, Paris, Rome and New York. So if you want authentic brand shopping at its five star best, this is your side of the street. Number 48 is the famous French run 'Fanny's' ice-cream parlor.

Carry on around the lake edge until you reach the other side of Hoan Kiem Lake. Then you will be walking along Dinh Tien Hoang Street.

ĐINH TIÊN HOÀNG

Dinh Tien Hoang was named after the emperor who vanquished twelve warlords. This heralded the Dinh Dynasty, which brought peace to the country in 968.

The lake you are walking around is one of the central points of Hanoi. Every morning, from 5.30am till 7am, Thai Chi and traditional fan dances are performed by the locals. This practice goes back to the time of the Le Dynasty, six centuries ago, when the legend of the lake was created.

Ask any local about the legend of the lake and the story they tell you, goes like this. During the war against the Chinese Minh Dynasty, the Vietnamese king, Le Thai To was given a magical sword by the Golden Turtle God from the lake in the middle of Hanoi, known as Luc Thuy, *green water*. After ten years of war, the King finally defeated the Chinese and reclaimed the nations independence.

Some time later, while the King Le Thai To was boating on Luc Thuy Lake, a large turtle swam towards him, took the sword, submerged and disappeared. The king realized that the Golden Turtle God of the lake must have presented the sword for the sole purpose of defeating the Chinese. In reverence, he named the Lake Ho Hoan Kiem or Lake of the Restored Sword. The Turtle Tower, *Thap Rua,* standing on a small island near the centre of the lake, is linked closely to the legend.

Towards the northern end of the lake, there's the ancient temple, Den Ngoc Son, Temple of the Jade Mountain. This temple honors the 13th century military leader Tran Hung Dao, who defeated the Mongols of the Yuan Dynasty. The island on which the temple sits is called Jade Island. To access the temple, you cross the red wooden Huc Bridge, *morning sunlight*. Picture postcard perfect; the red bridge, the jade water below, morning mist and peach blossoms.

Along Dinh Tien Hoang, there is a memorial park

on the right hand side of the road, called Ly Thai To Park. The golden statue of Ly Thai To, towers over the park and marble tiled square. Loudspeakers blast out dance music, early morning and in the evening for mass aerobic sessions. This is a chance to get together with a hundred Vietnamese doing aerobics in the park.

Carry on around the lake until you arrive back at the square near where you started. 'Thuy Ta' is a popular and friendly café restaurant, right on the lake's edge at number 1 Le Thai To Street. In summer, this cafe is a sanctury from the city heat. A fine mist of water vapor floats through the restaurant cooling the atmosphere. A great place to sit down and gaze across the lake as you relax after your walk.

FAT NOODLE'S 'VIETNAMESE STREET FOODIES GUIDE' IS A COMPANION FOR 'VIETNAM HANOI OLD QUARTER CITY WALKS'